STITCHING *in* *the* STACKS

STITCHING *in* *the* STACKS

Librarian-Inspired Knits

edited by

Sarah Barbour

COOPERATIVE PRESS
Cleveland, Ohio

Library of Congress Control Number: 2013940483
ISBN 13: 978-1-937513-23-8
First Edition

Published by Cooperative Press
http://www.cooperativepress.com

FOR COOPERATIVE PRESS

Senior Editor: Shannon Okey
Assistant Editor: Elizabeth Green Musselman
Technical Editors: Joeli Caparco, Ruth Garcia-Alcantud

Image on previous spread: Pack Horse Librarians in Boonesville, KY.
(Works Progress Administration, c.1936.)

TO THE PROTECTORS, ORGANIZERS,
AND DISTRIBUTORS OF KNOWLEDGE EVERYWHERE;

AND TO MY OWN THREE SEEKERS OF KNOWLEDGE,
SOPHIE, BLUE, AND IRENE.

Table of Contents

SECTION 1:
ARCHIVES—11

SECTION 2:
FICTION—61

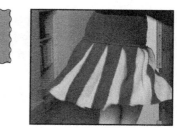

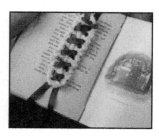

Preface

BY JESSAMYN WEST

One of the things that I was not prepared for when I started working in libraries was the prominent role that the weather would play in my professional life. I know that books and humans often thrive in differing temperature ranges and ambient humidities, but I had somehow underestimated our abilities as consummate researchers and problem solvers to regulate our environments. Authorities we can control, but thermostats and HVAC systems are often a mystery.

photo by Ben DeFlorio

I have worked in libraries where there was no way to turn the furnace off and we begged the management for an amendment to the "no shorts" rule in the summertime. I have worked in libraries that needed the air conditioning running 24/7 just so the basement did not become an accidental mossarium. I have been at staff meetings where the default status of the windows (open? closed? how far? when?) was a point of major and ongoing contention. I have seen librarians sneak behind other librarians' backs to adjust temperature settings.

It is in a library worker's best interests to be flexible about their own personal climate control systems. There is a reason the twinset is as much of a librarian convention as the bun and the sensible shoes: they're practical, especially when you're working someplace that may have a thirty-degree temperature swing in any given day. Linings are smart ideas for book jackets and for wool slacks.

I'm typing this in a pair of Jessamyn Mitts (see page III) from my rural treehouse in Vermont where the crisp outside autumn temperature pretty much matches the chilly inside temperature and my Yankee landlady resists turning on the furnace until October 1st—which is weeks from now—tenant law be damned. Did I mention library workers are often thrifty? We keep the temperatures low if we can, because the books like it. And it turns out that the servers like it too.

When I went to library school there was a persistent rumor that the twenty-four hour computer lab on campus was warmed purely from the heat that came from the mainframes. As computers got smaller the lab got cooler, or maybe that's what they told us to get us to show up in hats and gloves so they wouldn't have to turn up the heat. I have a question in to the University of Washington librarians about whether this was actually a true story. All I know is that I've typed in gloves before and glove technology has improved since the last century in both fashion and function.

Knitting is a thing I know less about. I am good at counting but bad at remembering, and anything more complicated than a knit-one/purl-two scarf sends me into a swivet of dread and unraveling. I am impressed by people with the knack, which, unless my eyes deceive me, includes a great number of my colleagues. A local librarian pal here raises Navajo-Churro sheep and sells beautiful wools when she's not in charge of multimedia storage and retrieval and lending at a local college. And ALA Council meetings always contained the *click click* of knitting needles long before they were joined by the *click click* of laptops.

So please enjoy this collection of fun, fashionable and functional designs for your favorite library worker, reader, laptopper or yarn enthusiast. Everyone can use something lovely to warm the heart and excite the eye. Happy stitching.

Introduction: Why This Book?

BY SARAH BARBOUR

Is there really a special connection between librarians and knitting?

Stereotypically, of course, librarians knit. They also wear glasses, keep cats, and put their hair up in buns. But I've known enough cat-less, spiky haired librarians with 20/20 vision to put too much faith in stereotypes.

Still, the circumstantial evidence of a link is persuasive: Ravelry's RaveLibrarians' group has more than 2,400 members; a growing number of libraries host knitting groups; recently, the American Library Association began hosting "CraftCons" at its conferences, where attendees can connect with fellow crafters; and in a survey of more than 1,500 librarians conducted by Stephen Abram, needlecraft was listed in the top ten most popular hobbies. (1)

Not only are a fair number of librarians knitters, but knitters are drawn to libraries. For knitters of all levels, libraries are a natural place to look for patterns, technical help, and inspiration—and they're more common than yarn stores. As knitting has surged in popularity over the past decade, libraries have increased their collections of knitting books, some even offering classes and knitting circles as a way of appealing to their communities.

As knitting has gained in popularity, the amount of knitting-related information has increased exponentially. Online discussion groups, instructional videos, and craft blogs have teamed up with traditional books and magazines to give knitters unprecedented access to information about every aspect of their craft. It shouldn't be surprising that information professionals might be drawn to this explosion of data and especially to "meta sites" such as Ravelry and Craftsy that make it more organized and accessible. Ravelry, in particular, is a crafting librarian's dream. An article in the library journal

InCite called it a "brilliant example of cataloguing/ describing, user contribution, and intelligent system design working together to create a useful, educational, and most importantly well-used … resource." (1)

But maybe the connection between librarians and knitting is a more fundamental one: just as knitters love to share their love of knitting, their mastery of a new stitch, and the esoterica of their craft, librarians also master a subject, share their knowledge, and find connections with people who speak their language. Maybe the connection lies in a mutual appreciation for preserving knowledge and sharing it.

The collection of patterns in this book is designed to celebrate that connection, whatever its cause. Each of the designs comes with its own fragment of library lore intended to educate, amuse, and enrich. Some of the patterns draw their inspiration from librarians themselves, from the famous to the fictional, to the obscure and anonymous. Others recall library architecture, cataloging systems, and sometimes the books themselves. It's my hope that the collection as a whole will be enjoyed by knitters of all stripes, because while not all librarians knit and not all knitters are librarians, it's not too much of a stretch to say that we all love libraries.

(1) Abram, Stephen. "Librarian Hobbies!! Here are the Results." *Stephen's Lighthouse*. Oct. 2010. Web. <http://stephenslighthouse.com/2010/10/31/librarian-hobbies-here-are-the-results/>

(2) Parkes, Nyssa. "FibreFRBRisation." *InCite* vol. 32, no. 11 (Nov. 2011), p. 23. <http://researchbank.swinburne.edu.au/vital/access/manager/Repository/swin:25095>

SECTION 1: ARCHIVES

BELLE GREENE
BY NINA MACHLIN DAYTON

She knows more about rare books than any other American.... She wears her hair long and does not use glasses, runs to Europe on secret missions, and is the terror of continental collectors' agents. Her name is Belle Greene.

—*Chicago Tribune*, August 11, 1912

Born in 1879, daughter of the first African-American man to graduate from Harvard, Belle da Costa Greene never received a formal degree herself. Nonetheless, her first job was at the Princeton University library, where she developed a fascination for medieval books.

In 1905, J. Pierpont Morgan, one of the wealthiest men in the world, hired her to catalog his growing collection of rare manuscripts. Witty, flirtatious, and always well dressed, Belle was perfectly at home in the world of wealth and glamour. She quickly earned her employer's trust, and was soon making regular trips to Europe where she negotiated on Morgan's behalf, dodged forgeries and tariff collectors, and developed professional, social, and romantic relationships with some of the most influential people of her time. She served as director of The Pierpont Morgan Library (now The Morgan Library & Museum) from 1924 until her retirement in 1948, and was instrumental in creating one of the world's most important collections of artistic, literary, and musical works.

Nina Dayton's Belle Greene shawl incorporates two lace patterns that were popular during the Gilded Age in which Belle began her remarkable career. Easily made larger or smaller, the shawl can be customized to fit the needs of the individual knitter. It has beads—the always stylish Belle would have appreciated a bit of sparkle—and provides just enough warmth to keep the chill off the shoulders of any librarian, or library patron, browsing in the stacks.

SIZE
One size

FINISHED MEASUREMENTS
Wingspan: 70" / 178cm
Length: 22" / 56cm
See Pattern Notes for instructions on changing shawl size.

MATERIALS
String Theory Caper Sock [80% merino wool, 10% cashmere, 10% nylon; 400 yds / 366m per 113g skein]; color: Black Cherry; 2 skeins

24-inch (or longer) US #6 / 4mm circular needle, or size needed to obtain gauge

Seed beads (384 total, size 6/0)

- Please note that this number does not include any extras to compensate for unusable beads. It is highly recommended that you buy more than the required amount so as to have extras.

Crochet hook small enough to fit into your beads
4 stitch markers
Yarn needle

GAUGE
Approx 17 sts and 25 rows = 4" / 10cm in St st, after blocking

14 sts and 16 rows = 4" / 10cm in Little Bud Lace pattern, after aggressive blocking

Differences in gauge will affect the finished size of the shawl and the yardage used, but are not crucial to fit.

PATTERN NOTES
To make the shawl larger or smaller, increase or decrease the Little Bud lace section reps by any even number of rows. The Beaded Lace knitted-on lace edging uses up (binds off) 2 sts for every 4-row rep, so for every additional (or fewer) 2 rows of the Little Bud Lace pattern, work 2 more (or fewer) reps of the lace edging chart. Increasing the size of the shawl will increase the yardage of yarn used and the number of beads needed.

All charts show RS and WS rows. Except where noted on Edging Set Up Row chart, all odd-numbered rows are RS rows and all even-numbered rows are WS rows.

All RS rows on charts are read from right to left and all WS rows are read from left to right.

Inc3: (K1, yo, k1) into next stitch.

If working primarily from charts, work as follows: Use written instructions for garter stitch tab and stockinette portion, then work Rows 1–12 of Little Bud Lace chart five times, then work Row 1 once more. Then work Edging Set-up Row chart once, and work Beaded Lace Edging chart 128 times until all sts from the body are used up. BO all rem sts purlwise.

PATTERN

Garter Stitch Tab Start:
CO 2 sts. Work in garter stitch (knit every row) for 10 rows (5 ridges).

Next Row: K 2 sts along top edge of rectangle. Turn work 90 degrees and pick up 5 sts along long edge of rectangle. Turn work 90 degrees; pick up 2 sts along short edge of rectangle. 9 sts.

Row 1: K2, inc3, yo, [K1, yo] 3 times, inc3, k2. 17 sts.
Row 2: K3, purl to last 3 sts, K3.
Row 3: K2, inc3, knit to last 3 sts, inc3, k2. 21 sts.
Row 4: K3, purl to last 3 sts, k3.
Rows 5–60: Rep rows 3 & 4 another 28 times. 133 sts.

If working from charts see Pattern Notes.
If working from written instructions proceed as follows:

Little Bud Lace Section:
Row 1 (RS): K2, inc3, k2, [yo, cdd, yo, k3] to last 8 sts, yo, cdd, yo, k2, inc3, k2.
Row 2 (WS): K3, [p2tog, p1, p2tog, yo, p1, yo] to last 8 sts, p5, k3.
Row 3: K2, inc3, k2, yo, cdd, yo, [k3, yo, cdd, yo] to last 3 sts, inc3, k2.
Row 4: K3, p3, [yo, p1, yo, p2tog, p1, p2tog] to last 3 sts, k3.
Row 5: K2, inc3, [yo, cdd, yo, k3] to last 6 sts, yo, cdd, yo, inc3, k2.
Row 6: K3, p4, [p2tog, p1, p2tog, yo, p1, yo] to last 6 sts, p3, k3.
Row 7: K2, inc3, yo, cdd, yo, [k3, yo, cdd, yo] to last 7 sts, k4, inc3, k2.
Row 8: K3, p1, [yo, p1, yo, p2tog, p1, p2tog] to last 7 sts, p4, k3.
Row 9: K2, inc3, k4, [yo, cdd, yo, k3] to last 4 sts, k1, inc3, k2.
Row 10: K3, p2, [p2tog, p1, p2tog, yo, p1, yo] to last 4 sts, p1, k3.
Row 11: K2, inc3, k1, [k3, yo, cdd, yo] to last 5 sts, k2, inc3, k2.
Row 12: K3, p5, [yo, p1, yo, p2tog, p1, p2tog] to last 5 sts, p2, k3.

Rep Rows 1–12 another 4 times, then rep Row 1 once more—257 sts.

LITTLE BUD LACE CHART

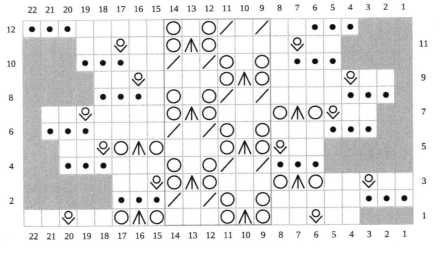

Legend:
- RS: Knit / WS: purl
- • RS: purl / WS: knit
- V RS: kfb / WS: pfb
- ∩ RS: Slip 1 / WS: Slip 1
- / RS: k2tog / WS: p2tog
- O RS: yo / WS: yo
- Λ RS: Cdd / WS: Cddp
- ⌢ RS: bind off knit wise / WS: bind off purl wise
- B p&b1 - purl and place bead
- inc3 - (k1, yo, k1) in 1 stitch
- no stitch
- Pattern repeat

14

Beaded Lace Edging: The edging of this shawl is made using a knitted-on edging, which is knit perpendicular to the body of the shawl. At the end of every WS (even-numbered) row, starting with the Set-up Row, there is a p2tog which works together 1 st from the edging with 1 st from the body of the shawl, attaching the two together. Each rep of the 4-row edging patt binds off 2 sts from the body.

Without breaking the yarn, CO an additional 19 sts at the end of the last row. Turn work, and continue working only on these 19 sts, except for the p2tog, which takes in 1 body st on each WS row.

Edging Set-up Row (WS): P3, p&b1, p5, p&b1, p8, p2tog.

Row 1 (RS): Sl1, k3, yo, k2tog, [k1, yo, k2tog, k1, k2tog, yo] twice, kfb.

Row 2 (WS): P3, yo, cddp, yo, p1, p&b1, p1, yo, cddp, yo, p4, yo, p2tog, p1, p2tog (1 st from the lace edging sts & 1 st from the body of the shawl). Turn work.

Row 3 (RS): Sl1, k3, [yo, k2tog, k1, k2tog, yo, k1] twice, yo, k3, kfb.

Row 4 (WS): BO 4 sts, yo, p1, p&b1, p1, yo, cddp, yo, p1, p&b1, p1, yo, p2tog, p2, yo, p2tog, p1, p2tog (1 st from the lace edging sts & 1 s from the body of the shawl). Turn work.

Work these 4 rows of the Beaded Lace Edging 128 times, until all body sts are used up.

FINISHING

BO all edging sts purlwise.
Cut yarn and weave in ends.
Wet block to desired finished measurements.

EDGING SET-UP ROW CHART

Set-up Row (WS)			B				B												/
19	18	17	16	15	14	13	12	11	10	9	8	7	6	5	4	3	2	1

	RS: Knit WS: purl
•	RS: purl WS: knit
V	RS: kfb WS: pfb
⋒	RS: Slip 1 WS: Slip 1
/	RS: k2tog WS: p2tog
O	RS: yo WS: yo
∧	RS: Cdd WS: Cddp
⌒	RS: bind off knit wise WS: bind off purl wise
B	p&b1 - purl and place bead
⚲	inc3 - (k1, yo, k1) in 1 stitch
▨	no stitch
	Pattern repeat

BEADED LACE EDGING CHART

HYPATIA
BY RACHEL ERIN

The last librarian of the Great Library of Alexandria was also the first notable woman in mathematics, as well as a philosopher, an astronomer, and a teacher. Born in the middle of the 4th century A.D., Hypatia was educated in Athens and later became head of the Platonist school of Alexandria.

Unfortunately, Hypatia lived at a time of political and religious turmoil. During her lifetime, part of the Great Library was destroyed by order of the Archbishop of Alexandria, and she herself met an unpleasant end at the hands of a mob in 415 A.D. Nonetheless, she has remained an inspiration for scientists and philosophers as well as novelists and playwrights for centuries.

Inspired by the ease and grace of classical clothing, Rachel Erin designed this airy silk and linen top in honor of Hypatia. The pullover is worked in a simple vertical lace stripe, which gradually converts to ribbing to form gentle waist shaping while the neckline decreases are all worked at the shoulder to make a graceful drape over the bust. It is the perfect layer over dresses or summer tops when the air conditioning is up too high in the library or the sea breezes turn cold at sunset while you gaze at the stars.

SIZES
Women's XS [S, M, L, XL, 2XL] (shown in size S)

FINISHED MEASUREMENTS
Chest: 28 [31.5, 35, 38.75, 45.75, 49.25]" / 71 [80, 89, 98.5, 116, 125]cm
Length: 14 [14, 14.25, 14.5, 14.75, 15]" / 35.5 [35.5, 36, 37, 37.5, 38]cm

MATERIALS
Handmaiden Flaxen [65% silk, 35% linen; 273.4 yds / 250m per 100g skein]; color: Smoke; 3 [4, 4, 4, 5, 6] skeins

US #5 / 3.75mm needles, or size needed to obtain gauge
2 double-point needles in same size as above
US 11 crochet hook, or size needed to fit through beads

Beads (50 total, 7 × 5 oval)
Bead threader
6 stitch holders (2 very small)
Yarn needle
Cotton crochet thread in matching color for seaming (optional)

GAUGE
21.5 sts and 29 rows = 4" / 10cm in St st, after blocking
18 sts and 27 rows = 4" / 10cm in Lace Stripe

PATTERN NOTES
Lace Edging (multiple of 2 sts + 3)
Row 1 (RS): K1, [k2tog, yo] to last 2 sts, k2.
Row 2 (WS): P1, [p2tog, yo] to last 2 sts, p2.

Lace Stripe (multiple of 4 sts + 1)
Row 1 (RS): K1, [k2tog, yo, k2] to end.
Row 2 (WS): P1, [p2tog, yo, p2] to end.

3 × 2 Ribbing (multiple of 5 sts + 6)
Row 1 (RS): K2, [p2, k3] to last 4 sts, p2, k2.
Row 2 (WS): P2, [k2, p3] to last 4 sts, k2, p2.

Place Bead: Thread bead on crochet hook. Grab the next stitch with hook, and slip bead onto stitch. Place stitch on RH needle without knitting.

Slip Bead: Using yarn with pre-threaded beads, slip a bead between two stitches.

Notes on increasing/decreasing in lace pattern: If there are not enough sts at the edge to work both a yarn over and its corresponding decrease, work in St st instead. Make sure that every yo is paired with a decrease.

Customization: It is easy to lengthen or shorten this sweater. Determine the total number or rows you would like to add or subtract. Add or subtract half this number of rows to the "work even" section before the ribbing, and between the ribbing and the armscye. Make sure you note how many rows you've changed, so you do the same thing to both the front at the back.

Due to the hand-painted nature of the yarn, I recommend alternating skeins throughout to prevent any obvious color shifts between sections.

PATTERN

BACK

Using the backwards loop cast on, CO 65 (73, 81, 97, 105, 121) sts. Work 4 rows in Lace Edging.

Switch to Lace Stripe. Work even for 12 (12, 12, 22, 24, 26) rows.

Next row (RS): Work 30 (34, 38, 46, 50, 58) sts in patt, pfb into the yo, k3, pfb into the yo, work in patt to end. 2 sts inc'd—67(75, 83, 99, 107, 123) sts total.
Next row (WS): Work patt as est, working k2 into the pfb on the wrong side.
Work 2 more rows even, in patt as est.

Sizes XS, S, M, L only:
Inc Row 1 (RS): Work to 4 sts before first purl column, pfb into yo, work in patt to next yo column, pfb into yo, cont in Lace Stripe to end—2 sts inc'd.

On the WS work in patt and work k2 into the pfb on the wrong side.

Rep Inc Row 1 every 4th row, 6 (5, 4, 1, 0, 0) more times—81 (87, 93, 103, 107, 123) sts.

Sizes S, M, L, XL, 2XL only:

Inc Row 2 (RS): Work to 8 sts before first purl st, pfb, k3, pfb, [k3, p2] to end of ribbing, pfb, k3, pfb, cont in Lace Stripe to end – 4 sts inc.

On the WS work in patt and work k2 into the pfb on the wrong side.

Rep Inc Row 2 every 4th row 0 (0, 1, 4, 5, 5) more times—81 (91, 101, 123, 131, 147) sts total. All lace columns are now converted to ribbing.

All sizes:
Work even in 3x2 ribbing for 6 rows.

Sizes S, M, L, XL, 2XL only:
Dec Row 1 (RS): Work to 1 st before first purl column, [ssk, yo, ktog, k2] twice, k1, work ribbing to 1 st before the second to last purl column, [ssk, yo, ktog, k2] twice—4 sts dec'd.

Rep Dec Row 1 every 4th row 0 (0, 1, 4, 5, 5) more times, working new yo columns in Lace Stripe—81 (87, 93, 103, 107, 123) sts total.

Sizes XS, S, M, L only:
Dec Row 2 (RS): Work to 1 st before first purl column, ssk, yo, k2tog, work in ribbing to 1 st before the last

purl column, ssk, yo, k2tog, cont in Lace Stripe as est to end—2 sts dec'd.

Rep Dec Row 2 every 4th row 6 (5, 4, 1, 0, 0) more times, working new yo columns in Lace Stripe—67 (75, 83, 99, 107, 123) sts.

***

Work Dec Row 2 once more. All purl columns are now converted back to yo columns—65 (73, 81, 97, 105, 121) sts total.

Work 10 (10, 12, 12, 12, 12) rows in Lace Stripe.

Keeping first and last 4 (4, 8, 8, 8, 8) sts in St st, work 2 more rows in Lace Stripe.

ARMHOLE SHAPING
BO 3 (3, 3, 4, 6, 8) sts at beg of foll 2 rows—59 (67, 75, 79, 93, 105) sts.

Dec Row (RS): K1, ssk, work in patt to last 3 sts, k2tog, k1.
Rep Dec Row 0 (0, 0, 3, 7, 7) more times—57 (65, 73, 81, 77, 89) sts.

Work even for 36 (36, 40, 42, 40, 38) rows.

BACK NECK
Next Row (RS): Work 21 (25, 29, 29, 33, 33) sts, place on holder, BO 15 (15, 15, 23, 23, 33) sts, work to end.

LEFT SHOULDER
Row 1 (WS): Work in patt.
Row 2: K1, ssk, work to end.
Row 3: Work in patt to last 3 sts, ssp, p1.
Rep Rows 2–3 once more—17 (21, 25, 25, 29, 29) shoulder sts.

Shape shoulder with short rows as follows:
Row 1: Work in patt until 5 sts rem on LH needle, w&t.
Row 2: Work in patt to end.
Row 3: Work in patt until 4 sts rem before the last wrapped st, w&t.
Row 4: Work in patt to end.
Rep the last 2 rows 2 (3, 4, 4, 4, 4) more times. Work 1 WS row.

Next Row (RS): Work in patt to end, picking up wraps as you come to them.
Next Row (WS): Purl.
Cut yarn and place sts on holder.

RIGHT SHOULDER

Rejoin yarn with WS facing.

Row 1 (WS): Work in patt to end.

Row 2 (RS): Work in patt to last 3 sts, k2tog, k1.

Row 3: P1, p2tog, work in patt to end.

Rep the last 2 rows once—17 (21, 25, 25, 29, 29) shoulder sts.

Row 1: Work in patt to end.

Row 2 (WS): Work in patt until 4 sts rem, w&t.

Row 3: Work in patt to end.

Row 4: Work in patt until 4 sts rem before the wrapped st, w&t.

Rep the last 2 rows 2 (3, 4, 4, 4, 4) more times. Work 1 WS row.

Next Row (RS): Work in patt to end, picking up wraps as you go.

Next Row (WS): Purl all sts and place on holder.

FRONT

Work as back until ***. Two purl columns rem in the center of the front.

All sizes:

Work 14 (14, 16, 16, 16, 16) rows in patt as est.

Keeping first and last 4 (4, 8,8,8,8) sts in St st, work 2 more rows in Lace Stripe.

ARMHOLE SHAPING

BO 3 (3, 3, 4, 6, 8) sts, work 30 (34, 38, 45, 47, 53) sts. Place Bead on next st (center st) and work to end.

BO 3 (3, 3, 4, 6, 8) sts at the beg of the foll row—61 (69, 77, 91, 95, 107) sts.

String rem beads onto one skein of yarn, to be used in the neckline.

Next row (RS): Using yarn with pre-stranded beads, k1, ssk, work in patt to center st, place sts on holder— 30 (34, 38, 45, 47, 53) sts on holder. M1 and work in patt to last 3 sts, k2tog, k1—30 (34, 38, 45, 47, 53) working sts.

RIGHT FRONT

Next row & all WS rows: Work in patt to last 4 sts, k2, p2. On the RS, every 4th row work a bead row: Sl 2, p1, slide bead, p1, cont in patt to end.

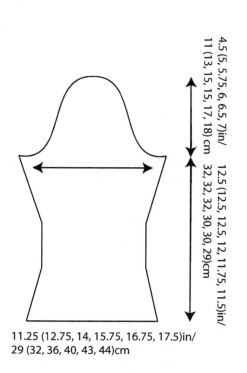

4.5 (5, 5.75, 6, 6.5, 7)in/ 11 (13, 15, 15, 17, 18)cm

12.5 (12.5, 12.5, 12, 11.75, 11.5)in/ 32, 32, 32, 30, 30, 29)cm

11.25 (12.75, 14, 15.75, 16.75, 17.5)in/ 29 (32, 36, 40, 43, 44)cm

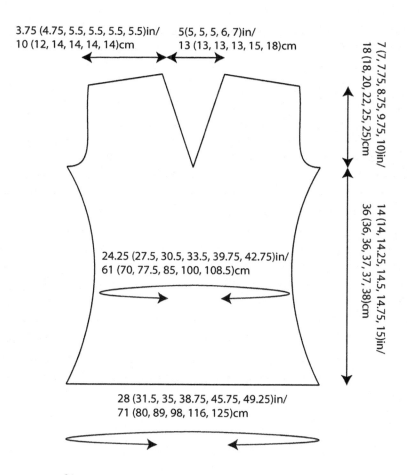

3.75 (4.75, 5.5, 5.5, 5.5, 5.5)in/ 10 (12, 14, 14, 14, 14)cm

5(5, 5, 5, 6, 7)in/ 13 (13, 13, 13, 15, 18)cm

7 (7, 7.75, 8.75, 9.75, 10)in/ 18 (18, 20, 22, 25, 25)cm

14 (14, 14.25, 14.5, 14.75, 15)in/ 36 (36, 36, 37, 37, 38)cm

24.25 (27.5, 30.5, 33.5, 39.75, 42.75)in/ 61 (70, 77.5, 85, 100, 108.5)cm

28 (31.5, 35, 38.75, 45.75, 49.25)in/ 71 (80, 89, 98, 116, 125)cm

Sizes L, XL, 2XL only:
Dec Row: Work in patt to last 3 sts, k2tog, k1—1 st dec'd.
Work Dec Row every RS row –(–, –, 3, 3, 7) times.

All sizes:
30 (34, 38, 42, 44, 46) sts for Right Front.
While completing the armhole decs if necessary, work even at the neck edge for 44 (48, 50, 54, 58, 60) rows.

Pleat Decrease Row (RS): Sl 2, p2, [k2tog] 4 (2, 2, 6, 2, 5) times, [k2tog, k2] 4 (6, 6, 6, 8, 7) times, k2tog, k0 (0, 4, 0, 2, 2)—21 (25, 29, 29, 33, 33) sts rem.
Next Row (WS): Purl to last 4 sts, k2, p2.

Place the first 4 sts on the neck edge on a small st holder for the edging.

Place rem 17(21, 25, 25, 29, 29) sts on a holder, to be joined to the back shoulder.

LEFT FRONT
Continue to use the yarn with the pre-stranded beads. Join the ball at the neck edge with the WS facing.

Next row and all WS rows: Sl 2, k2, work in patt to end. On the RS, every 4th row work a bead row: Work in patt to last 4 sts, p1, sl bead, p1, k2.

Sizes L, XL, 2XL only:
Dec Row: Work in patt to last 3 sts, k2tog, k1—1 st dec'd.
Work Dec Row every RS row 0 (0, 0, 3, 3, 7) times.

All sizes:
30 (34, 38, 42, 44, 46) sts for Left Front.
While completing the armhole decs if necessary, work even at the neck edge for 44 (48, 50, 54, 58, 60) rows.

Pleat Decrease Row (RS): [K2tog] 4 (2, 2, 6, 2, 5) times, [k2tog, k2] 4 (6, 6, 6, 8, 7) times, k2tog, k0 (0, 4, 0, 2, 2) p2, k2—21 (25, 29, 29, 33, 33) sts rem.
Next Row (WS): Sl 2, k2, purl to end.

Place the first 4 sts on the neck edge on a small stitch holder. Place rem 17 (21, 25, 25, 29, 29) sts on a holder, to be joined to the back.

SLEEVES
Using backward loop cast on, CO 45 (49, 53, 57, 61, 69) sts. Work 24 rows in Lace Edging.

Switch to Lace Stripe. Work 22 rows even. If you wish to lengthen or shorten the sleeves, add or subtract rows here.

Inc Row: K1, m1, work in patt to last st, m1, k1—2 sts inc'd.

Work Inc Row every 0 (10, 8, 6, 0, 6) rows 0 (3, 4, 2, 0, 3) more times, then every, 12 (8, 6, 4, 4, 4) rows, 2 (0, 0, 4, 6, 4) times—51 (57, 63, 71, 75, 85) sts.

Work 8 (6, 6, 10, 12, 2) rows even.
Keeping first and last 4 (4, 8, 8, 8, 8) sts in St st, work 2 more rows in Lace Stripe.

UNDERARM
BO 3 (3, 3, 4, 6, 8) sts at beg of foll 2 rows—45 (51, 57, 63, 63, 69) sts.

Dec Row (RS): K1, ssk, cont in patt to last 3 sts, k2tog, k1—2 sts dec'd.
Rep Dec Row every RS row 6 (5, 6, 6, 5, 4) more times, then every 4th row 1 (3, 3, 4, 6, 8) times, then every 6th row 6 (5, 6, 5, 4, 3) times—17 (23, 25, 31, 31, 37) sts total.

BO 3 (6, 8, 8, 5, 10) sts at beg of foll 2 rows. BO rem 11 (11, 13, 15, 15, 17) sts.

FINISHING
Block pieces to measurements, opening up the lace and making edges straight for seaming.

Join the shoulder seams with the three-needle bind off, leaving the 4 edge sts on each side of the front on their holders.

Starting at the underarm, set sleeves in sleeve cap, putting any ease at the shoulder. Seam sides, matching the patt changes (e.g. line up the ribbing at the waist first, and the underarm) and work from the matched points out.

Neckline: starting at the right shoulder, place saved edge sts on dpn. *Bring yarn to WS of work. Pick up (but do not knit) 1 st from the neck edge with the left side of the dpn. K2, p1, p2tog. Rep for 3 rows. Every 4th row, K2, p1, slip bead, p2tog. Rep the last 4 rows around the neckline. When picking up from the bound-off edge, pick up with the bind off to the RS of the work.

The tightness with which you knit the edging will determine how frequently you should pick up a stitch: if your neckline seems to be pulling and tight, pick up more a stitch more frequently. If it seems saggy or loose, pick up fewer. In the sample the pick up was approx 2 sts for every 3 rows, and 1 st for every 2 bound off sts.

Weave in ends. Block or steam entire sweater again to make seams even.

MAN OF LETTERS

BY MOLLY KENT

Man of Letters is inspired by the life and work of Benjamin Franklin, the quintessential "man of letters." Famous as a statesman, writer, scientist and inventor, Franklin also founded The Library Company of Philadelphia, the first lending library in America. Earlier libraries had been either private collections or the property of colleges. Beginning in 1731, however, the Library Company made books available to anyone who was able to pay the annual subscription fee of 10 shillings. Franklin's idea caught on and subscription libraries soon dotted the Atlantic coast, making a significant contribution to the intellectual climate of Colonial America.

The Library Company of Philadelphia is still in existence today, and is the repository of one of the most significant collections of historically valuable manuscripts in the United States.

Molly Kent's tribute to Franklin is worked in three simply shaped pieces; the colorwork is worked in intarsia. A skeleton key—a nod to Franklin's most famous experiment—is worked in purl stitches at the back collar. The recommended yarn, Shelter by Brooklyn Tweed, is an all-American wool to reflect Mr. Franklin's loyalties.

SIZES
Men's S [M, L, XL] (shown in size S)

FINISHED MEASUREMENTS
Chest: 38 [42, 46, 50]" / 96.5 [106.5, 117, 127]cm; designed to fit with 2" / 5cm of positive ease
Length (actual): 25 [26, 27, 27.8]" / 63.5 [66, 68.5, 70.5]cm

MATERIALS
Brooklyn Tweed Shelter [100% wool; 140 yds / 128m per 50g skein]
- [MC] Pumpernickel; 3 skeins
- [CC1] Nest; 3 skeins
- [CC2] Woodsmoke; 1 skein
- [CC3] Soot; 1 skein
- [CC4] Faded Quilt; 1 skein

1 set US #8 / 5.5mm needles, or size needed to obtain gauge
1 set US #7 / 4.5mm needles

2 stitch holders or scrap yarn
2 stitch markers
7 [7, 8, 8] ¾-inch buttons
Yarn needle

GAUGE
15 sts and 20 rows = 4" / 10cm in St st on larger needles

PATTERN NOTES
Pattern is written for size Small, instructions for other sizes are enclosed in (parentheses). If a number appears only once, it applies to all sizes.

Unless otherwise indicated, all work is done in St st.

A note on selvedge stitches: There are 2 selvedge stitches on the side-seam edge, and a single selvedge stitch on the button-band edge. The button-band selvedge stitches for sizes S, M and XL are in column A; those for size L are in column B (see chart). The side-seam selvedge stitches do not overlap on the chart, and are marked separately for each size. To reduce the number of yarn ends to be woven in, the selvedge stitches may be worked in the current "live" color even if the color chart indicates a color change; in other words, it doesn't matter what color the selvedge stitches are.

PATTERN

RIGHT FRONT
On larger needle and CC1, CO 4 sts. These 4 sts correspond to the rows marked by arrows on the color chart.

Hem shaping: For sizes S & L begin with a WS row; for sizes M & XL begin with a RS row. *Work 2 Hem Increase Rows. Work 1 row without incs. Rep from * until you have 26 (30, 36, 38) sts (including selvedge sts).

Hem Increase Row: Work 1, m1, work to last st, m1, work 1.

Sizes S, M, XL only:
Work 1 more row without incs.

Torso:
Torso Increase Row 1 (RS): Knit to last st, m1, k1.
Torso Increase Row 2 (WS): P1, m1, purl to end of row.

Work 12 (12, 15, 12) rows in color patt without increasing.
Work an inc row.
Work 12 (13, 16, 16) rows in patt.
Work an inc row.
Work 12 (13, 16, 16) rows in patt.
Work an inc row.
Work 12 (13, 16, 16) rows in patt.
Work an inc row.
Work 12 (13, 18, 23) rows in patt.

Sizes S, M only:
Work an inc row.
Work 12 (14) rows in patt.

Armhole shaping:
All decs are worked on WS rows.

Size S only:
BO 6 sts (including 2 selvedge sts) at beg of Row 78.
Knit Row 79.
BO 2 sts at the beg of Row 80.
Knit Row 81.
BO 2 sts at the beg of Row 82.
Knit Row 83.
P1, p2tog at the beg of Row 84.
Knit Row 85.
P1, p2tog at the beg of Row 86.
Knit Row 87.
P1, p2tog at the beg of Row 88.
Work in patt without decreasing through Row 100.

Size M only:
BO 6 sts (including 2 selvedge sts) at beg of Row 84.

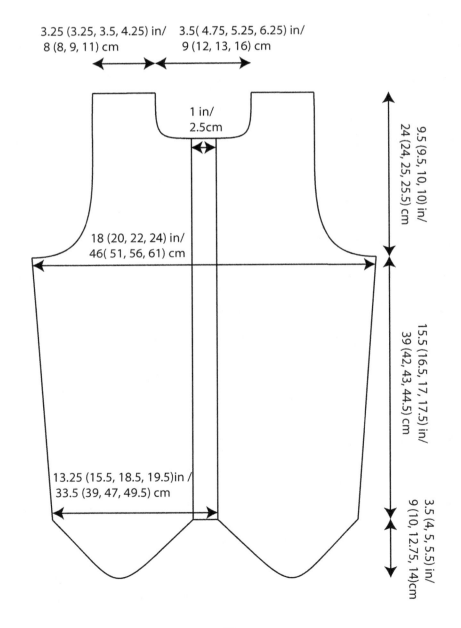

3.25 (3.25, 3.5, 4.25) in/
8 (8, 9, 11) cm

3.5 (4.75, 5.25, 6.25) in/
9 (12, 13, 16) cm

1 in/
2.5cm

9.5 (9.5, 10, 10) in/
24 (24, 25, 25.5) cm

18 (20, 22, 24) in/
46 (51, 56, 61) cm

15.5 (16.5, 17, 17.5) in/
39 (42, 43, 44.5) cm

13.25 (15.5, 18.5, 19.5)in /
33.5 (39, 47, 49.5) cm

3.5 (4, 5, 5.5) in/
9 (10, 12.75, 14)cm

Knit Row 85.
BO 3 sts at the beg of Row 86.
Knit Row 87.
BO 3 sts at the beg of Row 88.
Knit Row 89.
P1, p2tog at the beg of Row 90.
Knit Row 91.
P1, p2tog at the beg of Row 92.
Knit Row 93.
P1, p2tog at the beg of Row 94.
Work in patt without decreasing through Row 106.

Size L only:
BO 6 sts (including 2 selvedge sts) at beg of Row 86.
Knit Row 87.
BO 4 sts at the beg of Row 88.
Knit Row 89.
BO 2 sts at the beg of Row 90.
Knit Row 91.
BO 2 sts at the beg of Row 92.
Knit Row 93.
P1, p2tog at the beg of Row 94.
Knit Row 95.
P1, p2tog at the beg of Row 96.
Knit Row 97.
P1, p2tog at the beg of Row 98.
Knit Row 99.
P1, p2tog at the beg of Row 100.
Work in patt without decreasing through Row 108.

Size XL only:
BO 6 sts (including 2 selvedge sts) at beg of Row 88.
Knit Row 89.
BO 3 sts at the beg of Row 90.
Knit Row 91.
P1, p2tog at the beg of Row 92.
Knit Row 93.
P1, p2tog at the beg of Row 94.
Knit Row 95.
P1, p2tog at the beg of Row 96.
Knit Row 97.
P1, p2tog at the beg of Row 98.
Knit Row 99.
P1, p2tog at the beg of Row 100.
Knit Row 101.
P1, p2tog at the beg of Row 102.
Work in patt without decreasing through Row 110.

Neck shaping:
All decs are worked on RS rows.

Size S only:
BO 2 sts (including 1 selvedge st) at beg of Row 101.
Purl Row 102.
BO 2 sts at the beg of Row 103.
Purl to last 3 sts in Row 104, p2tog, p1.
K1, ssk, knit to end of Row 105.
Work in patt without decreasing through Row 124.

Size M only:
BO 3 sts (including 1 selvedge st) at beg of Row 107.
Purl Row 108.
BO 2 sts at the beg of Row 109.
Purl Row 110.
K1, ssk, knit to end of Row 111.
Purl Row 112.
K1, ssk, knit to end of Row 113.
Purl Row 114.
K1, ssk, knit to end of Row 115.
Work in patt without decreasing through Row 131.

Size L only:
BO 3 sts (including 1 selvedge st) at beg of Row 109.
Purl Row 110.
BO 2 sts at the beg of Row 111.
Purl Row 112.
K1, ssk, knit to end of Row 113.
Purl Row 114.
K1, ssk, knit to end of Row 115.
Purl Row 116.
K1, ssk, knit to end of Row 117.
Purl Row 118.
K1, ssk, knit to end of Row 119.
Work in patt without decreasing through Row 135.

Size XL only:
BO 3 sts (including 1 selvedge st) at beg of Row 111.
Purl Row 112.
BO 2 sts at the beg of 113.
Purl Row 114.
BO 2 sts at the beg of 115.
Purl Row 116.
K1, ssk, knit to end of Row 117.
Purl Row 118.
K1, ssk, knit to end of Row 119.
Purl Row 120.
K1, ssk, knit to end of Row 121.
Purl Row 122.
K1, ssk, knit to end of Row 123.
Work in patt without decreasing through Row 138.

All sizes:
Place rem 12 (12, 13, 16) sts on a stitch holder or scrap yarn. Do not BO. Weave in yarn ends.

LEFT FRONT

On larger needles and with CC1, CO 4 sts. These 4 sts correspond to the rows marked by arrows on the color chart.

Hem shaping: For sizes S & L begin with a WS row, for sizes M & XL begin with a RS row. *Work 2 inc rows. Work 1 row without incs. Rep from * until you have 26 (30, 36, 38) sts, including selvedge sts.

Sizes S, M, XL only: work 1 more row without incs.

Torso:
Torso Increase Row 1 (RS): K1, m1, knit to end of row.
Torso Increase Row 2 (WS): Purl to last st, m1, p1.

Work 12 (12, 15, 12) rows in color patt without increasing.
Work an inc row.
Work 12 (13, 16, 16) rows in patt.
Work an inc row.
Work 12 (13, 16, 16) rows in patt.
Work an inc row.
Work 12 (13, 16, 16) rows in patt.
Work an inc row.
Work 12 (13, 17, 22) rows in patt.

Sizes S, M only:
Work an inc row.
Work 11 (13) rows in patt.

Armhole shaping:
All decs are worked on RS rows.

Size S only:
BO 6 sts (including 2 selvedge sts) at beg of Row 77.
Purl Row 78.
BO 2 sts at the beg of Row 79.
Purl Row 80.
BO 2 sts at the beg of Row 81.
Purl Row 82.
K1, ssk at the beg of Row 83.
Purl Row 84.
K1, ssk at the beg of Row 85.
Purl Row 86.
K1, ssk at the beg of Row 87.
Work in patt without decreasing through Row 99.

Size M only:
BO 6 sts (including 2 selvedge sts) at beg of Row 83.
Purl Row 84.
BO 3 sts at the beg of Row 85.
Purl Row 86.
BO 3 sts at the beg of Row 87.
Purl Row 88.

K1, ssk at the beg of Row 89.
Purl Row 90.
K1, ssk at the beg of Row 91.
Purl Row 92.
K1, ssk at the beg of Row 93.
Work in patt without decreasing through Row 105.

Size L only:
BO 6 sts (including 2 selvedge sts) at beg of Row 85.
Purl Row 86.
BO 4 sts at the beg of Row 87.
Purl Row 88.
BO 2 sts at the beg of Row 89.
Purl Row 90.
BO 2 sts at the beg of Row 91.
Purl Row 92.
K1, ssk at the beg of Row 93.
Purl Row 94.
K1, ssk at the beg of Row 95.
Purl Row 96.
K1, ssk at the beg of Row 97.
Purl Row 98.
K1, ssk at the beg of Row 99.
Work in patt without decreasing through Row 107.

Size XL only:
BO 6 sts (including 2 selvedge sts) at beg of Row 87.
Purl Row 88.
BO 3 sts at the beg of Row 89.
Purl Row 90.
K1, ssk at the beg of Row 91.
Purl Row 92.
K1, ssk at the beg of Row 93.
Purl Row 94.
K1, ssk at the beg of Row 95.
Purl Row 96.
K1, ssk at the beg of Row 97.
Purl Row 98.
K1, ssk at the beg of Row 99.
Purl Row 100.
K1, ssk at the beg of Row 101.
Work in patt without decreasing through Row 109.

Neck shaping:
All decs are worked on WS rows.

Size S only:
BO 2 sts (including 1 selvedge st) at beg of Row 100.
Knit Row 101.
BO 2 sts at the beg of Row 102.
Knit to last 3 sts in Row 103, k2tog, k1.
P1, p2tog, purl to end of Row 104.
Work in patt without decreasing through Row 124.

Size M only:
BO 3 sts (including 1 selvedge st) at beg of Row 106.
Knit Row 107.
BO 2 sts at the beg of Row 108.
Knit Row 109.
P1, p2tog, purl to end of Row 110.
Knit Row 111.
P1, p2tog, purl to end of Row 112.
Knit Row 113.
P1, p2tog, purl to end of Row 114.
Work in patt without decreasing through Row 131.

Size L only:
BO 3 sts (including 1 selvedge st) at beg of Row 108.
Knit Row 109.
BO 2 sts at the beg of Row 110.
Knit Row 111.
P1, p2tog, purl to end of Row 112.
Knit Row 113.
P1, p2tog, purl to end of Row 114.
Knit Row 115.
P1, p2tog, purl to end of Row 116.
Knit Row 117.
P1, p2tog, purl to end of Row 118.
Work in patt without decreasing through Row 135.

Size XL only:
BO 3 sts (including 1 selvedge st) at beg of Row 110.
Knit Row 111.
BO 2 sts at the beg of 112.
Knit Row 113.
BO 2 sts at the beg of 114.
Knit Row 115.
P1, p2tog, purl to end of Row 116.
Knit Row 117.
P1, p2tog, purl to end of Row 118.
Knit Row 119.
P1, p2tog, purl to end of Row 120.
Knit Row 121.
P1, p2tog, purl to end of Row 122.
Work in patt without decreasing through Row 138.

All sizes:
Place rem 12 (12, 13, 16) sts on a stitch holder or scrap yarn. Do not BO. Weave in yarn ends.

BACK
On smaller needles and with MC, CO 52 (58, 70, 74) sts. Work 2 (3, 3, 4) rows in [k1, p1] rib. Change to larger needles, and knit 1 row, increasing 4 (6, 6, 6) sts across the row. 56 (64, 76, 80) sts.

Torso shaping:
Work 11 (12, 14, 15) rows.
Inc 1 st at each edge of the foll row.
Rep these 12 (13, 15, 16) rows 5 (5, 4, 4) more times—68 (76, 86, 90) sts.
Work 3 (2, 6, 3) additional rows without increasing.
If your last row was a WS row, continue to armhole shaping. If your last row was a RS row, work 1 additional row.

Armhole shaping:
Size S only:
BO 6 sts at the beg of the foll 2 rows.
Dec 2 sts at either end of the foll 2 alternating rows.
Dec 1 st at either end of the foll 3 alternating rows—42 sts.

Size M only:
BO 6 sts at the beg of the foll 2 rows.
BO 3 sts at the beg of the foll 4 rows.
Dec 1 st at either end of the foll 3 alternating rows—46 sts.

Size L only:
BO 6 sts at the beg of the foll 2 rows.
BO 4 sts at the beg of the foll 2 rows.
BO 2 sts at the beg of the foll 4 rows.
Dec 1 st at either end of the foll 4 alternating rows—50 sts.

Size XL only:
BO 6 sts at the beg of the foll 2 rows.
BO 3 sts at the beg of the foll 2 rows.
Dec 1 st at either end of the foll 6 alternating rows—60 sts.

All sizes:
On foll row, place markers to designate the center 8 sts. Beg on the foll (RS) row, work the Key Chart over the marked sts.

Bobble: Knit into front and back 3 times. Slip 5 sts one at a time over the last worked st.

Work 11 (14, 11, 12) rows.
Next row: Work 12 (12, 13, 16) sts, BO until 12 (12, 13, 16) sts rem, work to end of row.
Work 3 (3, 4, 4) rows on either side of the neck.

FINISHING

With right sides together, work a 3-needle BO across the shoulder sts to attach the two front pieces to the back. Sew side seams.

*With smaller needles and CC1, pick up and knit 99 (105, 108, 110) sts along right front edge. Work 7 rows in [k1, p1] rib. BO in patt.

Rep from * on left edge, working 7 (7, 8, 8) evenly spaced buttonholes (see below) in the 4th row.

Sew buttons onto right side band.

One-row self-reinforcing buttonhole:
Bring yarn to front of work, slip 1, return yarn to back of work. Slip 1, pass first slipped st over. Rep until desired number of sts have been cast off (test your buttons on a swatch to determine the required number). Slip the last bound-off st back to the LH needle. Turn work. Using the cable cast on, CO the number of sts that you just bound off, plus one. Before you place the last cast-on st onto the LH needle, bring the working yarn to the front, between the needles. Turn work. Slip the first st from the LH needle to the RH needle, pass the extra cast-on stitch over this slipped st.

With smaller needles and CC1, pick up and knit with right side facing around the edge of the armhole. BO all sts in purl. Rep on other arm hole.

With smaller needles and CC1, pick up and knit with right side facing around the collar. BO all sts in purl.

Weave in yarn ends and block to size.

KEY CHART

	knit
●	purl
B	make bobble

RIGHT LOWER FRONT

- ◼ MC
- ◼ CC1
- % CC2
- ◆ CC3
- # CC4
- ☐ Small
- ☐ Medium
- ☐ Large
- ☐ X-Large
- ☐ Selvedge stitch

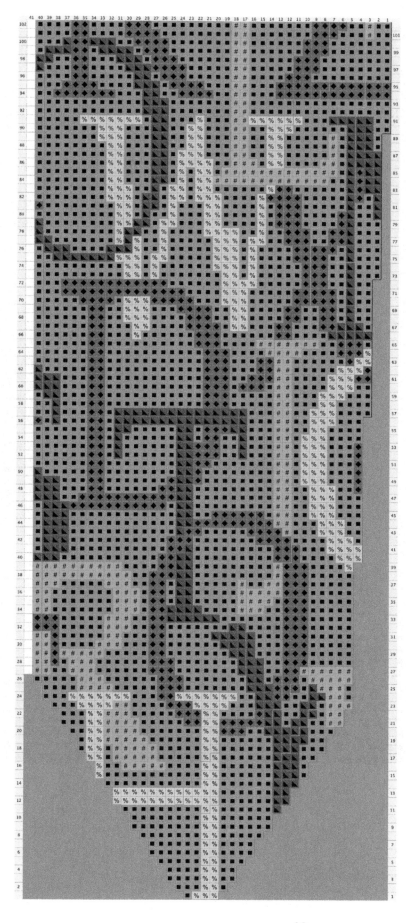

LEFT LOWER FRONT

◪ MC

▪ CC1

% CC2

◆ CC3

CC4

□ Small

□ Medium

□ Large

□ X-Large

□ Selvedge stitch

RIGHT UPPER FRONT

- ◼ MC
- ◼ CC1
- % CC2
- ◆ CC3
- # CC4
- ☐ Small
- ☐ Medium
- ☐ Large
- ☐ X-Large
- ☐ Selvedge stitch

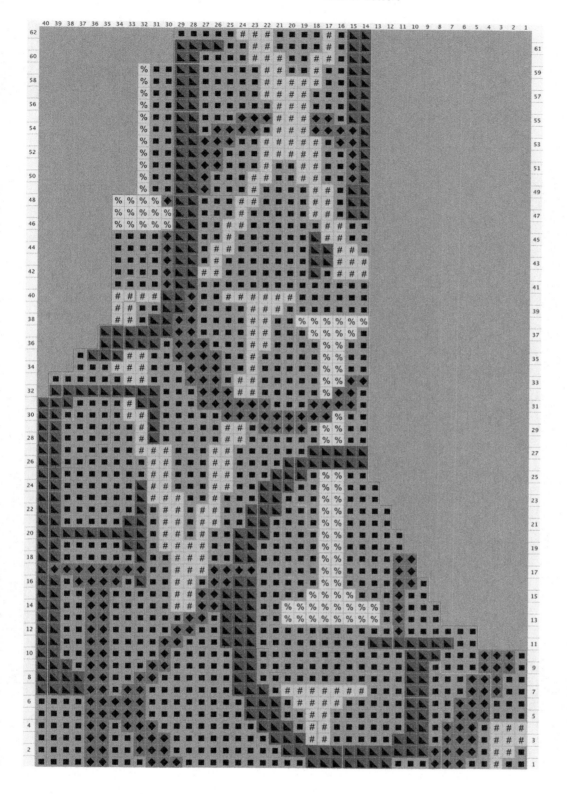

LEFT UPPER
FRONT

■ MC

■ CC1

% CC2

◆ CC3

CC4

☐ Small

☐ Medium

☐ Large

☐ X-Large

☐ Selvedge stitch

RANGANATHAN'S MITTS
BY SHARON FULLER

Books are for use
Every reader his book
Every book its reader
Save the time of the reader
The library is a growing organism

These are the Five Laws of Library Science, proposed in 1931 by S. R. Ranganathan, an Indian mathematician and librarian who is considered one of the founders of modern library and information science. His "laws" focus on creating libraries that serve patrons, rather than staff or administrators, and have acted as a cornerstone of library science ever since. Ranganathan's birthday is still observed in India every August 9 as National Library Day.

Sharon Fuller designed these mitts as a reminder of what—and whom—libraries are for. Wearing a law on the back of each hand, a librarian can proclaim her (or his) fealty to the profession while keeping hands warm for typing or shelving books.

SIZES
Women's M [women's L/men's S, men's M]
(shown in the smaller two sizes)

FINISHED MEASUREMENTS
Circumference: 7.5 [8, 8.5]" / 19.5 [20, 21.5]cm
Length: 6 [6.25, 6.5]" / 15 [16, 16.5]cm

MATERIALS
St Denis Boreale [100% wool; 225yds / 206m per 50g ball]
- [MC] #1278 Bison; 1 ball
- [CC] #1236 Oatmeal; 1 ball

You will have enough yarn to make two pairs of mitts if you reverse MC and CC for the second pair.

US #1 / 2.25mm circular needle or 1 set double-point needles, or size needed to obtain gauge
US size C / 2.75mm crochet hook

5 split-ring stitch markers
Yarn needle
Waste yarn

GAUGE
34 sts and 36 rnds = 4" / 10cm in colorwork patt

PATTERN NOTES
Ribbed Cable Cast On:
A ribbed cable cast on is the same as a regular cable cast on except that it is worked in one by one ribbing.

Set-up (2 sts cast on):
Make a slip knot and place loop over LH needle. This counts as a knit st, so the next st will be cast on in purl. Insert RH needle through first st and purl. After each st is made, sl that st back to LH needle.

- *Insert RH needle from front to back between last 2 sts on LH needle; k1.
- Insert RH needle from back to front between last 2 sts on LH needle; p1.
- Rep from *, alternating knit and purl sts, until desired number of sts have been cast on.

To keep track of whether the next cast-on st should be knit or purled, remember that the side of the LH needle from which the yarn is hanging is the side from which to insert your needle for the next st.

Backward Loop Cast On:
Loop working yarn and place it on needle backward so that it doesn't unwind. Rep until desired number of sts have been cast on.

Purl Cast On:
This cast on is recommended for the extra thumb sts because the cast-on sts are easy to pick up. The purl cast on is exactly the same as the knit cast on, except that it is done in purl. Purl first st from LH needle and sl new st back to LH needle. Rep until desired number of sts have been cast on.

Short Row Wrap and Turn (w&t):
Wrap and Turn

- (RS): Knit to st to be wrapped, yf, sl 1, yb, turn; sl this st at beg of foll row.
- (WS): Purl to st to be wrapped sl 1, yb, turn; sl this st at beg of foll row.

Work st together with wrap:

- If head of wrap is to left of st: Slip st to RH needle, use LH needle to lift wrap on to RH needle, slip both loops back to LH needle and k2tog.
- If head of wrap is to right of st: Use RH needle to lift wrap, place it on LH needle to the left of the wrapped st and skp.

Single Crochet (sc):
To work single crochet into a rnd of live knit sts:

- Holding yarn in left hand, insert hook knitwise through first st, place yarn over hook from right to left and bring through the st (1 loop on hook).
- *Rep step 1 (2 loops on hook). Place yarn over hook and pull the yarn through the two loops on the hook. Rep from * to end.

Chain (ch):
With one loop on crochet hook, place yarn over hook from right to left and pull yarn through loop.

Slip Stitch (sl st):
With one loop on crochet hook, insert hook through another st, place yarn over hook and pull yarn through both loops.

PATTERN

Where more than one number is listed, first number is for smallest size, and numbers in brackets are for larger sizes. Where only one number is listed, it applies to all sizes.

CUFF

Using ribbed cable cast on (see Pattern Notes), CO 58 (62, 66) sts in CC. Break CC.

Turn work and knit one row with MC, starting from beg of cast on.
Join to work in the round, being careful not to twist.

Work cuff in twisted rib as follows:
Rnd 1: Cont in MC, sl 1, k1tbl, [p1, k1tbl] around.
Rnd 2: [P1, k1tbl] around.
Rep Rnd 2 until cuff is about 2" / 5cm or desired length.

HAND
Work chart. Pm at middle of rnd as shown on chart.

Notes:

- On each rnd, work MC and CC where indicated on chart. Yarn that is not used for a st is carried loosely (floated) behind the work.
- Carry CC below MC so that CC sts will be more prominent.
- If a color is not used for more than three or four sts in a row, catch it occasionally with working yarn to avoid long floats.
- To avoid tight floats at ends of needles, turn work inside out and work across back needle.
- To keep the edges of gusset pattern neat, work inc sts for gusset using backward loop cast on (see Pattern Notes).
- At top of thumb gusset, slip the 19 (21, 23) thumb sts to waste yarn when you reach them. As shown on chart, use purl cast on (see Pattern Notes) to CO 5 sts to cover the gap.

Size Women's Medium only:

- Left hand: Break CC after Rnd 20 and re-join at Rnd 22.
- Right hand: Break CC after Rnd 23 and re-join at Rnd 24.

For the last 5 rnds of the chart, you can follow either the chart or these equivalent written instructions. All markers are placed in fabric between sts to mark edges of fingers. If you want to finish the finger edges with CC, switch to CC for the final rnd.

Both hands:
Row 1: Knit to 7 (8, 8) sts before middle of row, pm, wrap next st and turn (w&t; see Pattern Notes).
Row 2: Purl to beg of row. Cont purling on back needles to last 7 (8, 8) sts before middle of row, w&t.

Left hand:
Row 3: Knit to beg of row. Cont knitting on back needles to last 15 (16, 17) sts before middle of row, pm, w&t.
Row 4: Purl to beg of row. Cont purling on palm needles to last 14 (15, 16) sts before middle of row, w&t.
Row 5: Knit to beg of row.
Final row: (Switch to CC if desired.) Sl 1, k2tog, pm, skp, k7 (8, 8), pm; knit to 2 sts before middle of row, knitting wrapped sts tog with their wraps; k2tog, sl m, skp; knit to end of rnd, working wrapped sts tog with their wraps using skp.

Right hand:

Row 3: Knit to beg of row. Cont knitting on palm needles to 14 (15, 16) sts before middle of row, pm, w&t.

Row 4: Purl to beg of row. Cone purling on back needles to last 15 (16, 17) sts before middle of row, w&t.

Row 5: Knit to beg of row.

Final rnd: (Switch to CC if desired.) Sl 1, k4 (5, 5), pm; knit to 2 sts before middle of row, knitting wrapped sts tog with their wraps; k2tog, sl m, skp; knit to 5 sts before end of rnd, working wrapped sts tog with their wraps using skp; k2tog, pm, skp, k1.

TOP EDGE

See Pattern Notes for crochet techniques. If you prefer not to use crochet, you can substitute a purl bind off for the sc, and instead of doing the crochet chain across: CO 3 sts, pick up one st from other side of glove, and BO new sts.

If you worked the final rnd in CC, use CC for the edge; otherwise use MC.

Left hand:

Shift beg of rnd 2 sts to the left by knitting first 2 sts and shifting to palm needle. Starting from the new beg of rnd, work one sc into each live st across back needles to middle-of-rnd marker.

- Little Finger: Sc 6 (7, 7), ch2, sl st into back edge between little and ring fingers at marked location, sl st 2 back into the first 2 ch sts.
- Ring Finger: Sc 7 (7, 8), ch2, sl st into back edge between ring and middle fingers, sl st back as for little finger.
- Middle Finger: Sc 8 (8, 9), ch2, sl st into back edge between middle and index fingers, sl st back.
- Index Finger: Sc rem 7 (8, 8) sts.

Right hand:
Work one sc into each live st across palm needles to middle-of-rnd marker.

- Little Finger: Sc 6 (7, 7) sts, chain (ch) 2, slip stitch (sl st) into palm edge between little and ring fingers at marked location, sl st 2 back into the first 2 ch sts.
- Ring Finger: Sc 8 (8, 9), ch2, sl st into palm edge between ring and middle fingers, sl st back as for little finger.
- Middle Finger: Sc 8 (8, 9), ch2, sl st into palm edge between middle and index fingers, sl st back.
- Index Finger: Sc rem 10 (11, 11) sts.

After last st is worked, sl st under both loops of first sc. Break yarn and thread end through final loop to secure.

THUMB
Restore 19 (21, 23) thumb sts to needles from waste yarn.

Row 1: Using MC, leave a 10" / 25.5cm tail and knit across the restored sts to last st. Knit last st tog with adjoining cast-on st. Turn work.
Row 2: Purl to last st. Purl last st tog with adjoining cast-on st. Turn work.
Rnd 3: Knit around, picking up and knitting rem 3 cast-on sts at end of rnd. 22 (24, 26) thumb sts on needles.

Work sc around edge of thumb as for fingers.
Work second mitt.

FINISHING
Weave in ends and block.

WOMEN'S MEDIUM: LEFT HAND CHART

WOMEN'S MEDIUM: RIGHT HAND CHART

WOMEN'S LARGE / MEN'S SMALL: LEFT HAND CHART

WOMEN'S LARGE / MEN'S SMALL: RIGHT HAND CHART

MEN'S MEDIUM: LEFT HAND CHART

MEN'S MEDIUM: RIGHT HAND CHART

Knitting Typography

SHARON FULLER

There are nearly as many ways of incorporating text into knitted objects as there are knitting techniques. As I developed patterns for this book, I experimented with several techniques for creating the knitted word, and found that each can be used for good or ill, depending on the context.

I focus here on three colorwork techniques—stranded knitting, mosaic, and duplicate stitch—with particular attention to working on the smaller knitted "page." While intarsia and illusion knitting are also excellent ways of creating text using color (see the Mystery Novel Cover on page 89), those techniques are generally worked over more pixels, and can be treated in the same way as other graphic elements.

COLORWORK TECHNIQUES

In stranded knitting, two or more colors are worked per row, with the color not in use for a given stitch floated behind the work.

In mosaic knitting, only one color is worked per row, with stitches from the other color being slipped up from the previous row. Mosaic designs are generally quite geometric because of construction constraints imposed by the technique.

Duplicate stitch, or Swiss darning, is applied after the knitted fabric is complete by using a yarn needle and contrast color to trace the existing stitches.

CHOOSING COLORS

Regardless of the technique you use, color matters. For maximum legibility, pick colors with high contrast in value (i.e. light versus dark). In general, light and warm colors appear to advance, while dark and cool colors recede. Therefore, light colored text will typically appear more prominent against a dark background than dark text on a light background. On the other hand, dark letters on a light background have a more traditional look. Ranganathan's Mitts (page 37) provide a good example of both approaches.

FINDING AN ALPHABET

You can find knitting alphabets in printed stitch dictionaries and online. (Ravelry.com is an excellent resource.) Cross-stitch alphabets are even more abundant, both in pattern books and online.

Keep in mind that cross-stitch alphabets (and most knitting charts, for that matter) use square pixels. These can work reasonably well for stranded or mosaic knitting, which tend to have nearly equal stitch and row gauge. However, when your stitches are wider than they are tall (as they are in most knitting), using a square-based alphabet will lead to squat-looking text. You can avoid this by choosing a relatively elongated alphabet to begin with or, better yet, using knitter's graph paper to adapt an existing alphabet or create your own.

It is surprisingly easy to create your own letters, especially if you need only a small set. Creating an entire upper- and lower-case alphabet is more of an undertaking, but the most important skill required is patience. Well, patience and swatching. While developing the alphabets for Ex Libris (page 157), it was distressingly common for me to make a lovely chart that translated to gobbledygook on the knitted page.

CHOOSING A TECHNIQUE

When choosing a colorwork technique, consider the following:

DO YOU WANT TO USE LOWERCASE LETTERS?

Lowercase letters with ascenders and descenders are well suited to duplicate stitch, but would require prohibitively long floats in stranded knitting. Lowercase is possible in mosaic knitting (see fig. 1 on next page), but requires all-over patterning between rows of text.

HOW MANY STITCHES DO YOU HAVE AVAILABLE?

Given enough pixels, it is possible to build quite an elegant mosaic alphabet. If you have to work small, the construction rules for mosaic knitting yield odd-looking letters.

Stranded knitting is an apt choice for confined quarters, but duplicate stitch is the clear choice for legibility over the smallest number of stitches, because you can compress duplicate stitch letters by working over half stitches. With half stitches, you can also make smoother curves and add serifs.

In fig. 2, a duplicate stitch M is worked over just three stitches. In the following two images, half-stitches help define curves and serifs on a tilted P and a curvy S.

HOW LARGE WILL YOUR STITCHES BE?

In thin yarn worked at a tight gauge, single horizontal lines of stranded knitting may look a bit ephemeral. Duplicate stitch, on the other hand, may be bulky to the point of illegibility.

In fig. 5, a tight gauge yields nearly illegible duplicate stitch; an alpaca halo obscures the stranded knitting work; and the mosaic letters look awkward over a small number of stitches.

WHAT KIND OF YARN DO YOU PLAN TO USE?

Fuzzy yarn will obscure any text, especially if the letters are small, although you can choose to use that fact to create pleasingly blurred edges on larger designs. Conversely, smooth, tightly spun yarn may be challenging to use for duplicate stitch because the contrast stitches may not completely cover the underlying fabric.

For all three techniques, you should choose yarns of similar weights, but don't feel constrained to use the same yarn for every color. Unexpected combinations can produce striking results.

Mohair silk laceweight held doubled on merino silk sock yarn.

HOW FLEXIBLE IS YOUR DESIGN?

Duplicate stitch is a great choice if you want the freedom to experiment, because you don't have to design the text until after you know the exact size and shape of your knitted page and, if you make a mistake, it's easy to fix without ripping out fabric. Also, there are no constraints on the number of contrast colors you can use.

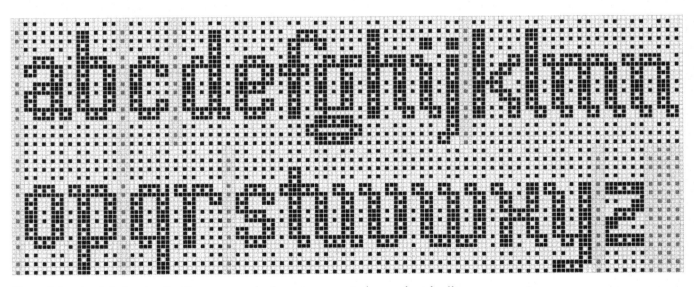

Fig. 1: Mosaic alphabet by Jay Petersen worked over many stitches and with all-over patterning.
©2008 Jay Petersen, fuzzyjay.blogspot.com.

DO YOU WANT ADDITIONAL PATTERNING?

With stranded or mosaic knitting, you must include patterning across the entire round to avoid excessive floats. Duplicate stitch is a poor choice for all-over patterning, because it quickly becomes tedious and may adversely affect the drape of your fabric. However, for a more spare design, duplicate stitch allows you to place text or other patterning exactly where you want it, and use only as much as you want.

WHAT KIND OF FABRIC DO YOU WANT?

Both mosaic and stranded knitting make a dense, firm fabric. Used sparingly, duplicate stitch has little effect on the qualities of the base fabric, although it does add surface texture. Used in large blocks, duplicate stitch will stiffen the fabric and can slightly distort stitch and row gauge.

HAVE YOU BLOCKED IT YET?

Before you decide a technique isn't working, block your fabric (fig. 5). 'Nuff said.

Top row: figs. 2, 3, 4. Bottom row: figs. 5, 6

CARNEGIE VEST
BY JAMES MAGEE

There is not such a cradle of democracy upon the earth as the Free Public Library, this republic of letters, where neither rank, office, nor wealth receives the slightest consideration.

—Andrew Carnegie

One of the most influential figures in the modern library system was not a librarian at all. As a boy, Andrew Carnegie fled poverty in Scotland for the textile mills of Pittsburgh. Through hard work and clever investments, he became one of the world's wealthiest men and one of the nation's greatest philanthropists.

Largely self-educated, he understood the difficulty that the working class had in accessing books, and he focused much of his philanthropic energies on libraries. He not only gave money to fund libraries in towns and cities across the United States, but also insisted on community involvement in them, requiring towns to donate the land on which he built the libraries and lobbying for ongoing funding through taxes.

Today more than 2,500 libraries throughout the world bear the name Carnegie so it seemed only fitting that we include a design with his name as well. James Magee's classic shape and modern colors pay tribute to a man who came from the Old World and helped shape the New.

SIZES
Men's S [M, L, XL, 2XL] (shown in size L)

FINISHED MEASUREMENTS
Chest: 36 [40, 44, 48, 52]" / 91.5 [101.5, 112, 122, 132]cm
Length: 23 [24.5, 25, 25.5, 26]" / 58.5 [62, 63.5, 64.5, 66]cm

MATERIALS
Ístex Léttlopi [100% wool; 109 yds / 100m per 50g skein]
- [MC] #9420 navy blue; 2 [2, 3, 3, 3] skeins
- [CC1] #1419 barley; 1 [1, 1, 2, 2] skein(s)
- [CC2] #9427 rust heather; 1 [1, 1, 2, 2] skein(s)
- [CC3] #9423 lagoon heather; 1 [1, 2, 2, 2] skein(s)
- [CC4] #1416 moor (dark green); 1 [1, 1, 2, 2] skein(s)
- [CC5] #9434 crimson red; 1 [1, 1, 1, 1] skein
- [CC6] #9418 stone blue heather (light blue); 1 [1, 1, 1, 1] skein
- [CC7] #9429 berry heather (purple); 1 [1, 1, 1, 1] skein

32-inch US #7 / 4.5mm circular needle, or size needed to obtain gauge
16-inch US #6 / 4mm circular needle (or longer circular for magic loop)

Cable needle or dpn (US #7 / 4.5mm)
Yarn needle
Stitch marker
Stitch holder

GAUGE
21 sts and 29 rnds or rows per 4" / 10cm, St st on larger needles

NOTES
Vest is worked in the round up to the armholes then worked back and forth. Ensure that your gauge does not change between the two sections. Many knitters find it necessary to decrease needle size when switching from working round to working flat.

Weave in ends as you go, either by carrying yarn ends double with same coloured working yarn or by weaving in ends as you would long yarn floats on the WS of stranded colorwork.

RCDD (right-leaning cable needle double decrease): Place the next 2 sts on a cable needle or dpn. Hold cable needle behind work. Insert needle into first st on main needle then first st on cable needle, knit these 2 sts tog. Rep—2 sts dec'd.

LCDD (left-leaning cable needle double decrease): Place the next 2 sts on a cable needle or dpn. Hold cable needle in front of work. Insert needle into first st on cable needle then first st on main needle, knit these 2 sts tog. Rep—2 sts dec'd.

Stripe sequence is as follows (46 rows total): 6 rows CC2, 1 row CC1, 6 rows CC3, 1 row CC1, 6 rows CC4, 1 row MC, 6 rows CC5, 1 row CC1, 3 rows CC3, 1 row CC1, 6 rows CC6, 1 row CC1, 6 rows CC7, 1 row MC.

PATTERN

BODY

Using MC and larger needles, CO 188 (208, 228, 252, 272) sts. Pm for start of rnd, join and work in the round.

Work in [k2, p2] ribbing for 12 (14, 14, 16, 16) rnds. Switch to CC1, work 1 rnd in St st.

Start stripe sequence (see Note 4) and continue in St st. When work measures 12.5 (13.5, 13.5, 13.5, 13.5)" / 32 (34.5, 34.5, 34.5, 34.5)cm from CO edge, work until last 6 (7, 9, 10, 13) sts of rnd. BO 12 (14, 18, 20, 26) sts, removing m. Work 82 (90, 96, 106, 110) sts as est. Place these Front sts on holder.

BO 12 (14, 18, 20, 26) sts. Knit next 81 (89, 95, 105, 109) sts to end. 82 (90, 96, 106, 110) sts on needles are Back sts.

BACK

From this point, garment is worked back and forth in St st instead of in the round. Turn work, purl across Back sts, turn work.

Back armhole dec row (RS): k1, ssk, knit to last 3 sts, k2tog, k1—2 sts dec'd.

Rep back armhole dec row 6 (7, 8, 11, 12) more times on every RS row—12 (14, 16, 22, 24) sts dec'd; 68 (74, 78, 82, 84) sts on needles.

Work straight until Back measures 19.5 (20.5, 21, 21.5, 22)" / 49.5 (52, 53.5, 54.5, 56)cm from CO edge, ending on a WS row and either 17 or 18 rows (19 or 20, 19 or 20, 19 or 20, 19 or 20) prior to the end of a 3- or 6-row stripe.

Shoulder Dec Row (RS): k2, RCDD, knit to last 6 sts, LCDD, k2—4 sts dec'd. Be sure to work k2 on either end loosely.

Rep Shoulder Dec Row 8 (9, 9, 9, 9) more times on every RS row—32 (36, 36, 36, 36) sts dec'd; 32 (34, 38, 42, 44) sts rem across Back.

If required, work one more WS row to finish 3- or 6-row stripe. Work 1 row in CC1 (whether on RS or WS), leaving approx 20" / 50cm of yarn on either end of the row. These ends will be used to seam the shoulder seams. Place Back sts on holder.

LEFT FRONT

Working with Front sts from holder and larger needles, attach appropriately coloured yarn to continue stripe sequence. On the RS, k41 (45, 48, 53, 55) from beg to center of Front sts. Rest of sts rem on holder to form Right Front. Turn work, purl across Left Front sts, turn work.

RS: k1, ssk (armhole dec), knit to last 3 sts, k2tog (V-neck dec), k1.

AT THE SAME TIME, rep armhole dec 6 (7, 8, 11, 12) more times on every RS row AND rep V-neck dec 15 (16, 18, 20, 21) more times on every other RS row.

At the end of the armhole dec, st count should be 30 (33, 34, 35, 35). At the end of the V-neck decreases, st count should be 18 (20, 20, 20, 20). Work straight until Left Front measures 24 (25.5, 26, 26.5, 27)" / 61 (64.5, 66, 67.5, 68.5)cm from CO edge, ending before a 1-row stripe.

RIGHT FRONT

Working with Right Front sts from holder and larger needles, attach appropriately coloured yarn to continue stripe sequence. Work straight across 41 (45, 48, 53, 55) sts, turn work, purl across Right Front sts, turn work.

RS: k1, ssk (V-neck dec), knit to last 3 sts, k2tog (armhole dec), k1.

AT THE SAME TIME, rep armhole dec 6 (7, 8, 11, 12) more times on every RS row AND rep V-neck dec 15 (16, 18, 20, 21) more times on every 2nd RS row.

At the end of the armhole decreases, st count should be 30 (33, 34, 35, 35). At the end of the V-neck decreases, st count should be 18 (20, 20, 20, 20). Work straight until Right Front measures 24 (25.5, 26, 26.5, 27)" / 61 (64.5, 66, 67.5, 68.5)cm from CO edge, ending before a 1-row stripe.

RIGHT SHOULDER SEAM

Shoulder seams are worked with a half-seam (on the shoulder dec selvedge) and half-graft (on the live Front sts) approach as follows.

Place Right Front sts on a dpn or rearrange circular needle so that sts are on the needle with the point on the right-hand side when looking at the RS (i.e. sts should be arranged as if to work on the RS). Using the long tail in CC1 from the Back, thread a blunt sewing needle. Hold work with shoulder selvedge on the top and Right Front sts on the bottom. Bring the yarn up from behind the shoulder selvedge edge, with a 1-st selvedge and between the last orange row and the oatmeal row. Bring yarn through first st on needle purlwise.

*Sew under next row to the left on the shoulder selvedge. Bring yarn through first st on needle knitwise. Drop st from needle. Bring yarn through next st on needle purlwise. Rep from * until all sts on needle have been dropped. Sew one more row from the shoulder selvedge.

LEFT SHOULDER SEAM
Place Left Front sts on a dpn or rearrange circular needle so that sts are on the needle with the point on the left-hand side when looking at the RS (i.e. sts should be arranged as if to work on the WS). Using the long tail in CC1 from the back, thread a blunt sewing needle. Hold work with shoulder selvedge on the bottom and Left Front sts on the top. Bring the yarn up from behind the shoulder selvedge edge, with a 1-st selvedge and between

the last orange row and the oatmeal row. Bring yarn through first st on needle knitwise.

*Sew under next row to the left on the shoulder selvedge. Bring yarn through first st on needle purlwise. Drop st from needle. Bring yarn through next st on needle knitwise. Rep from * until all sts on needle have been dropped. Sew one more row from the shoulder selvedge.

NECKBAND
Working with MC and smaller needles, and using a 1-st selvedge, start at the bottom center of the V-neck and pick up and k59 (62, 64, 66, 69) sts evenly along neckline of Right Front, k32 (34, 38, 42, 44) Back sts from holder, pick up and k59 (62, 64, 66, 69) sts evenly along neckline of Left Front down to center of V-neck—150 (158, 166, 174, 182) sts total.

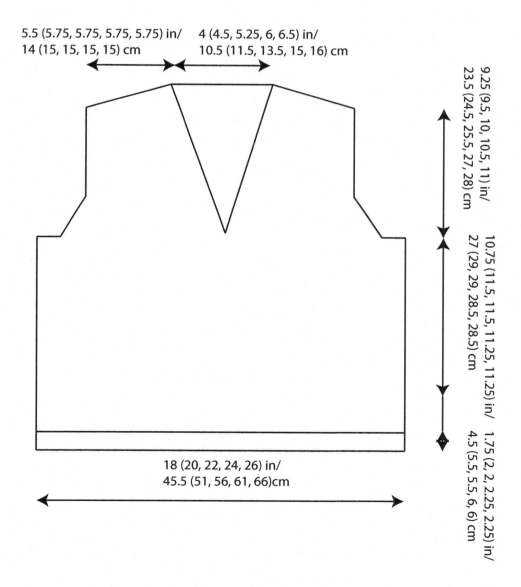

5.5 (5.75, 5.75, 5.75, 5.75) in/
14 (15, 15, 15, 15) cm

4 (4.5, 5.25, 6, 6.5) in/
10.5 (11.5, 13.5, 15, 16) cm

9.25 (9.5, 10, 10.5, 11) in/
23.5 (24.5, 25.5, 27, 28) cm

10.75 (11.5, 11.5, 11.25, 11.25) in/
27 (29, 29, 28.5, 28.5) cm

1.75 (2, 2, 2.25, 2.25) in/
4.5 (5.5, 5.5, 6, 6) cm

18 (20, 22, 24, 26) in/
45.5 (51, 56, 61, 66)cm

Do NOT join, turn, work [p2, k2] rib along WS, ending with a p2. Continue working [k2, p2] ribbing flat for 8 (8, 8, 10, 10) more rows.

BO all sts in patt.

LEFT ARMBAND
Working with MC and smaller needles, start at center of BO sts at underarm. Pick up and k6 (7, 9, 10, 13) sts to end of BO area. Using a 1-st selvedge, pick up and k58 (60, 62, 64, 68) sts evenly up the Left Front to the shoulder seam, then pick up and k34 (34, 36, 40, 42) sts evenly down Back. Pick up and k6 (7, 9, 10, 13) sts to center of BO area—104 (108, 116, 124, 136) sts total.

Join to work in the round. Work 1 rnd of [k2, p2] rib. Continue as est for 5 (6, 6, 7, 7) more rnds. BO all sts in patt.

RIGHT ARMBAND
Working with MC and smaller needles, start at center of BO sts at underarm. Pick up and k6 (7, 9, 10, 13) sts to end of BO area. Using a 1-st selvedge, pick up and k34 (34, 36, 40, 42) sts evenly up Back to the shoulder seam, then pick up and k58 (60, 62, 64, 68) sts evenly down the Right Front. Pick up and k6 (7, 9, 10, 13) sts to center of BO area—104 (108, 116, 124, 136) sts total.

Join to work in the round. Work 1 rnd of [k2, p2] rib. Continue as est for 5 (6, 6, 7, 7) more rnds. BO all sts in patt.

FINISHING
Perform last adjustments of tension on grafted seams at shoulders. Lay left end of Neckband over right and using MC yarn and a yarn needle, sew the selvedge of the left side to the first rnd on the right.

Weave in all ends.
Block garment to final dimensions.

BOOK WOMAN JACKET
BY SARAH BARBOUR

From 1935 to 1943, the Works Progress Administration of the US Government sponsored the Pack Horse Librarian Project. The object of this unusual program was two-fold: both to provide books to the rural population of Appalachia and to create jobs for women.

The Pack Horse Librarians, some as young as sixteen, earned $28 a month. Every week, snow, rain, or shine, they rode horses and mules over dozens of miles of rugged terrain to deliver books and magazines to remote homes and schools. Often they stayed to read to children, invalids, and illiterate adults, their visits and their books deeply appreciated by the poverty stricken population that they served. Known as the "Book Women" by their patrons, these dedicated librarians both supported their families and brought a glimpse of a wider world to their constituents.

After reading a fictionalized account of one book woman's exhausting ride over snowy slopes and through icy streams, Sarah Barbour decided to design a cold-weather jacket in honor of these rough-riding librarians. The gentle shaping and the cabled front with its inset buttonholes provide style, while the broad collar, double-vested front and cozy pockets will keep you warm, on horseback or off.

SIZES
XS [S, M, L, XL, 2XL] (shown in size XS)

FINISHED MEASUREMENTS
Chest: 38.25 [41.5, 46.75, 50, 55.25, 60.75]" / 97 [105.5, 119, 127, 140.5, 154.5]cm
Length: 18 [18, 19, 20, 22, 22]" / 45.5 [48, 50, 55.5, 55.5]cm

MATERIALS
Valley Yarns Berkshire [85% wool, 15% alpaca; 141 yds / 129m per 100g ball]; color: Tan Heather; 9 [9, 10, 12, 15, 18] balls

US #9 / 5.5mm circular needle, or size needed to obtain gauge
1 set US #9 / 5.5mm double-point needles
24-inch (or longer) US #8 / 5mm circular needle

6 stitch markers
Eight 1" buttons
2 stitch holders or scrap yarn
Cable needle
Yarn needle

GAUGE
15 sts and 27 rows = 4" / 10cm in stockinette stitch

PATTERN NOTES
Sweater is worked from the top down. The right panel is worked in cable pattern; the left in reverse stockinette stitch. Collar is picked up and knit, but could also be worked separately and sewn on. Vertical pockets are optional. Cuffs are meant to be worn doubled.

Buttonhole Instructions:
Yo twice, sl next 2 sts from LH needle to right purlwise, pull first st over second and off needle, sl next st from LH needle to right purlwise, pull second st over first one and off needle. Slip rem st back onto LH needle and purl. Next row (WS): work in patt to yarn overs, k1, ktbl, cont in patt.

Moss Stitch (worked over even number of sts):
Rows 1 & 2: [K1, p1] to end of row.
Rows 3 & 4: [P1, k1] to end of row.

M1L = make one left: With LH needle tip, lift strand between needles from front to back. Knit lifted loop through the back.

M1R = make one right: With LH needle tip, lift strand between needles from back to front. Knit lifted loop through the front.

See chart key for cable abbreviations.

PATTERN
YOKE
Using long-tail method and larger needles, CO 40 (42, 48, 60, 66, 64) sts.

Size XS: Purl 1 row, pm after 2nd, 8th, 32nd & 38th sts.
Size S: Purl 1 row, pm after 2nd, 8th, 34th, & 40th sts.

Size M: Purl 1 row, pm after 2nd, 10th, 38th, & 46th sts.
Size L: Purl 1 row, pm after 3rd, 13th, 47th, & 57th sts.
Size 1X: Purl 1 row, pm after 3rd, 15th, 51st, & 63rd sts.
Size 2X: Purl 1 row, pm after 3rd, 13th, 51st, & 61st sts.

Sizes XS–M only:
Row 1 (RS): *Knit to 1 st before m, m1R, k1, sl m, k1, m1L; rep from * to end of row—8 sts inc'd.
Row 2: Purl.

Sizes L–2X only:
Row 1 (RS): k1, m1R, [knit to 1 st before m, m1R, k2, m1L] to 1 st before end of row, m1L, k1. 10 sts inc.
Row 2: Purl.
Rep Rows 1 & 2 three more times.

All sizes:
There should be 72 (74, 80, 100, 106, 104) sts on the needles. From this point, make incs only at the raglan seams (not at the neckline), increasing 8 sts on every RS row.
Row 9 (RS): Pm and CO 22 (22, 22, 22, 36, 36) sts. [K2, p2] to first m, [knit to 1 st before m, m1R, k1, sl m, k1, m1L] to end of row—102 (104, 110, 130, 150, 148) sts.
Row 10: Pm and CO 32 (32, 32, 52, 52, 52) sts. K4, [p2, k2] to first m, purl to last m, [k2, p2] to end—134 (136, 142, 162, 202, 200) sts.

Begin cable section:
Row 1: Purl to first m, knit across with incs as est to last m, [p2, T3F, T3B, p2, k2, p6, k2] 1 (1, 1, 1, 2, 2) time(s), p2, T3F, T3B, p2, k2.
Row 2: K2, [k3, p4, k3, p2, k6, p2] 1 (1, 1, 1, 2, 2) time(s), k3, p4, k3, purl to last m, knit to end.

Row 3: K2, purl to first m, work in St st with incs as est to last m, [p3, C4B, p3, T3F, p4, T3B] 1 (1, 1, 1, 2, 2) time(s), p3, C4B, p3, k2.
Row 4: K2, [k3, p4, k4, p2, k4, p2, k1] 1 (1, 1, 1, 2, 2) time(s), k3, p4, k3, purl to last m, knit to end.

Row 5: Row 5: K2, purl to first m, work in St st with incs as est to last m, [p1, T4B, T4F, p2, T4F, T4B, p2] 1 (1, 1, 2, 2) time(s), T4B, T4F, p1, k2.
Row 6: K2, [k1, p2, k4, p2, k4, p4, k3] 1 (1, 1, 1, 2, 2) time(s), k1, p2, k4, p2, k1, purl to last m, knit to end.

Row 7: K2, purl to first m, work in St st with incs as est to last m, [T3B, p4, T3F, p3, C4B, p3] 1 (1, 1, 1, 2, 2) time(s), T3B, p4, T3F, k2.
Row 8: K2, [p2, k6, p2, k3, p4, k3] 1 (1, 1, 1, 2, 2) time(s), p2, k6, p2, purl to last m, knit to end.

Row 9: K2, purl to first m, work in St st with incs as est to last m, k2, p2, work buttonhole, p1, k2, p3, k4, p3 [sizes 1X and 2X only: *k2, p6, k2], k2, p2 work buttonhole, p2, k4.

Row 10: K2, [p2, k6, kfb into double yarn over, p2, k3, p4, k3] 1 (1, 1, 1, 1, 2, 2) time(s), p2, k6 kfb into double yarn over, p2, purl to last m, knit to end.

Row 11: K2, purl to first m, work in St st with incs as est to last m, [T3F, p4, T3B, p3, C4B, p3] 1 (1, 1, 1, 2, 2) time(s), T3F, p4, T3B, k2.
Row 12: Rep Row 6.

Row 13: K2, purl to first m, work in St st with incs as est to last m, [p1, T4F, T4B, p2, T4B, T4F, p1] 1 (1, 1, 1, 2, 2) time(s), p1, T4F, T4B, p1, k2.
Row 14: K2, [k3, p4, k4, p2, k4, p2, k1] 1 (1, 1, 1, 2, 2) time(s), k3, p4, k3, purl to last m, knit to end.

Row 15: K2, purl to first m, work in St st with incs as est to last m, [p3, C4B, p3, T3B, p4, T3F] 1 (1, 1, 1, 2, 2) time(s), p3, C4B, p3, k2.
Row 16: K2, [k3, p4, k3, p2, k6, p2] 1 (1, 1, 1, 2, 2) time(s), k3, p4, k3, purl to last m, knit to end.

Row 17: K2, purl to first m, work in St st with incs as est to last m, [p3, k4, p3, k2, p6, k2] 1 (1, 1, 1, 2, 2) time(s), p3, k4, p3, k2.

Continue working cabled Rows 2–17, working buttonholes only on every second rep. Simultaneously continue working incs until a total of 24 (26, 30, 30, 34, 38) inc rows have been worked, ending with a WS row—286 (304, 342, 362, 434, 464) sts.

DIVIDE FOR SLEEVES
Work in patt for 48 (51, 54, 58, 77, 81), skip 54 (60, 68, 74, 80, 86) sts, placing these on holder, work 72 (80, 88, 98, 104, 114) sts, skip 54 (60, 68, 74, 80, 86) sts, placing these on holder, work in patt to end.

Next row (WS): Keeping in patt, work 48 (50, 52, 55, 76, 82) sts, pm, work 28 (31, 32, 36, 43, 44) sts, pm, work 38 (40, 44, 52, 52, 56) sts, pm, work 28 (31, 32, 36, 43, 44) sts, pm, work to end.

Work 6 (6, 6, 6, 4, 4) rows even ending with a WS row. Work a dec row as foll every 4 rows 3 (4, 4, 4, 5, 6) times:
Dec row: [Work to 2 sts before m, k2tog, work to next m, sl m, ssk] twice, work to end in patt—162 (172, 190, 206, 254, 268) sts.

Work 12 (12, 12, 12, 14, 14) rows even ending with a WS row.

Beg next row, work an inc row as foll every 4 rows 2 times: Inc row: [Work to 1st m, m1, sl m, work to next m, sl m, m1L] twice, work to end in patt—178 (184, 206, 214, 274, 292) sts.

Work 1 row even.

Note: Pockets are optional. If you do not wish to work them, continue working inc rows every 4 rows an additional 6 times.

DIVIDE FOR POCKETS

The two fronts and the back will be worked separately then rejoined once the pockets are shaped. The extra sts cast on for the back section will form the pocket linings.

LEFT FRONT

Work to 1st m. Place rem sts on holder. Work in patt for one row. Next row (RS): Work inc row as foll: Work in patt to 2 sts before end, m1L, k1. Work inc row every 4 rows 6 times. Work 1 more row even, ending on a WS row. Break yarn and place left front sts on holder.

RIGHT FRONT

Remove sts from right side edge to 1st m from holder and place on needle. Join yarn at the pocket side and work 2 rows even. Next row (RS): Work inc row as foll: k1, m1R, work in patt to end. Work inc row every 4 rows

FRONT CHART

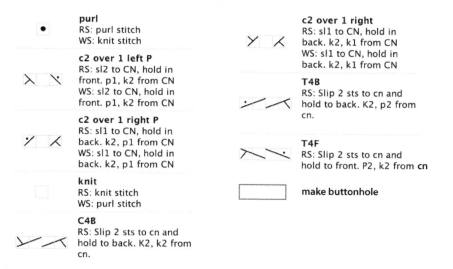

| | **purl**
RS: purl stitch
WS: knit stitch |
| • | |

| | **c2 over 1 left P**
RS: sl2 to CN, hold in front. p1, k2 from CN
WS: sl2 to CN, hold in front. p1, k2 from CN |

| | **c2 over 1 right P**
RS: sl1 to CN, hold in back. k2, p1 from CN
WS: sl1 to CN, hold in back. k2, p1 from CN |

| | **knit**
RS: knit stitch
WS: purl stitch |

| | **C4B**
RS: Slip 2 sts to cn and hold to back. K2, k2 from cn. |

| | **c2 over 1 right**
RS: sl1 to CN, hold in back. k2, k1 from CN
WS: sl1 to CN, hold in back. k2, k1 from CN |

| | **T4B**
RS: Slip 2 sts to cn and hold to back. K2, p2 from cn. |

| | **T4F**
RS: Slip 2 sts to cn and hold to front. P2, k2 from cn |

| | **make buttonhole** |

6 times. Work 1 more row even, ending on a WS row. Break yarn and place sts on holder.

BACK SECTION

Remove center sts from holder and place on needle. Join yarn on the right side. CO 28 sts at beg of foll 2 rows and work in St st.

Next row (RS): Work inc row as foll: k1, m1R, work in patt to last st, m1L, k1. Work inc row every 4 rows 6 times. Work 1 more row even, ending on a WS row. Break yarn and place all sts on holder.

REJOINING BODY

Join yarn at left front edge and work in patt for 16 (19, 22, 26, 44, 47) sts, overlap front sts with pocket lining sts and knit together, cont in patt across back, overlap first 28 sts of the right front over right pocket lining sts and knit together, cont in patt to end.

Work inc rows every 4 rows 2 (2, 2, 2, 3, 4) more times. 166 (168, 190, 198, 254, 268) sts. Work even in St st until jacket measures 18 (18, 19, 20, 22, 22)" / 45.5 (45.5, 48, 51, 56, 56)cm from back neck or to desired length.

Next WS row: K2, [p2tog, k4] 5 (5, 5, 5, 8, 8) times. Work in patt to end. Work in moss st for an additional 2.5" / 6.5cm.

SLEEVES

Place sleeve sts on dpns, dividing evenly over needles. Pm to mark beg of rnd.

Work 10 (8, 6, 5, 5, 4) rows.
Work 1 dec rnd as foll: K1, k2tog, knit to 3 sts before m, ssk, k1. Rep these rows 6 (8, 11, 14, 15, 19) more times—40 (42, 44, 44, 48, 46) sts. Work in moss st for 5.5" / 14cm.

COLLAR

Beg at top of left panel, pick up and knit 104 (104, 104, 104, 144, 144) sts. Work 3 reps (or to desired size) according to Collar Cable Chart.

FINISHING

Pick up and knit 18 sts along outer edge of each pocket opening. Work in moss st for 3 rows. Tack edges down.

Block. Sew buttons on to left front panel to correspond with buttonholes. Carefully sew sides and tops of pocket linings to sweater so that sts do not show. Weave in ends.

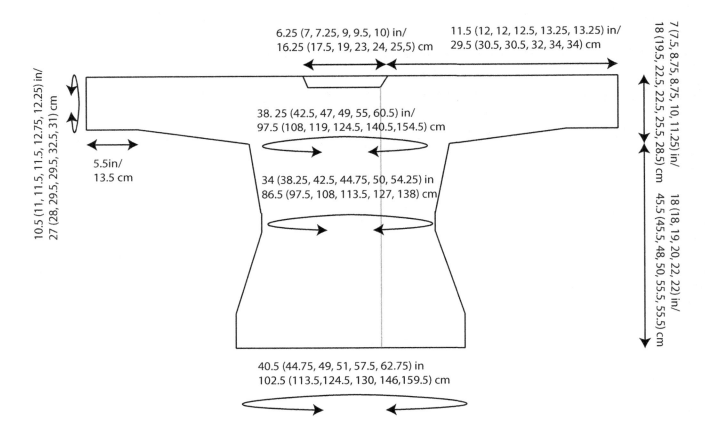

6.25 (7, 7.25, 9, 9.5, 10) in/ 16.25 (17.5, 19, 23, 24, 25,5) cm

11.5 (12, 12, 12.5, 13.25, 13.25) in/ 29.5 (30.5, 30.5, 32, 34, 34) cm

7 (7.5, 8.75, 8.75, 10, 11.25) in/ 18 (19.5, 22.5, 22.5, 25.5, 28.5) cm

10.5 (11, 11.5, 11.5, 12.75, 12.25) in/ 27 (28, 29.5, 29.5, 32.5, 31) cm

5.5in/ 13.5 cm

38. 25 (42.5, 47, 49, 55, 60.5) in/ 97.5 (108, 119, 124.5, 140.5,154.5) cm

34 (38.25, 42.5, 44.75, 50, 54.25) in 86.5 (97.5, 108, 113.5, 127, 138) cm

18 (18, 19, 20, 22, 22) in/ 45.5 (45.5, 48, 50, 55.5, 55.5) cm

40.5 (44.75, 49, 51, 57.5, 62.75) in 102.5 (113.5,124.5, 130, 146,159.5) cm

COLLAR CABLE CHART

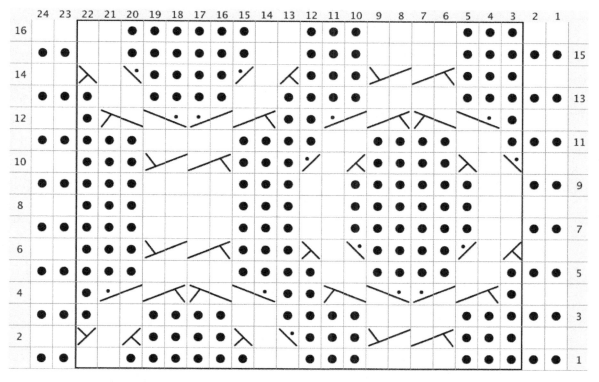

SECTION 2: FICTION

GOTHAM CITY TWINSET
BY SARAH BARBOUR

When Barbara Gordon was introduced to television and comic book audiences in 1967, her library career was merely a cover-up for her true identity as Batgirl. Later in the comic books her character became a paraplegic and her research skills came to the fore. She became known as Oracle, a computer genius and information broker. More recently, Barbara has regained the use of her legs and her Batgirl alter ego has been restored. It remains to be seen how this will affect her library career, but having been for decades one of the most popular female superheroes, there's little doubt that she will continue to surprise and inspire.

Sarah Barbour's short-sleeved pullover is worked from the top down with full-fashioned shaping to show off super-heroine curves. The coordinating shawl is worked with short rows to create the gradient, cape-like hem. Worn separately or as a dynamic duo, this twinset travels from the stacks to the streets with ease.

GOTHAM CITY CAPE

SIZE
One size

FINISHED MEASUREMENTS
Depth: 17" / 43cm
Outer circumference: 140" / 356cm

MATERIALS
Cascade Ultra Pima [100% cotton; 220 yds / 201m per 100g skein]; color: #3708 Regal; 4 skeins

US #5 / 3.5mm circular needle, or size needed to obtain gauge

One ½" button
Yarn needle

GAUGE
18 sts and 28 rows = 4" / 10cm in lace pattern

PATTERN NOTES
Shawl is worked from the top down. Short rows are used to make the back longer than the front, creating a "cape" effect.

Short Rows / Wrap and Turn (w&t)
- On RS, with yarn in front, slip next stitch to RH needle purlwise, bring yarn around this stitch to back of work, slip stitch back to LH needle, turn work.
- On WS, with yarn in back, slip next stitch to RH needle, bring yarn around this stitch to front of work, slip stitch back to LH needle, turn work.

PATTERN
CO 55 sts.
Knit 1 row.
Inc Row: K3, m1, knit to end.
Rep Inc Row 5 more times—61 sts.

Establish Patt (RS): K4, work Top Front Chart, k1, [work Top Main Chart, k1] 5 times, work Top Front, k4.
Next and all WS rows: K4, purl to last 4 sts, k4.
Cont in patt until Top Front Chart has been worked in full—173 sts.

Next RS row: K4, [work Main Chart, k1] 6 times, work Main Chart, k4.
Cont in patt for 31 more rows, ending after a WS row—397 sts.

Next RS row: Work Left Front Chart, k1, [work Main chart, k1] 5 times, work Right Front Chart.
Cont in patt until Left Front and Right Front Charts have been worked in full—493 sts.

SHORT ROW SHAPING
Short Row 1 (RS): K4, work in Main Chart patt up to 1 st before Right Front section, w&t.
Short Row 2 (WS): Purl to 1 st before Left Front section, w&t.
Short Row 3: Work to 1 st before wrapped st, w&t.
Work Short Row 3 another 17 times.

Short Row 4: Work in patt to 10 sts before wrapped st, w&t.
Work Short Row 4 another 3 times.

Short Row 5: Work in patt to 20 sts before wrapped st, w&t.

Work Short Row 5 once more.

Work in patt for 2 rows, picking up and working each wrapped st with its st as they appear.
Purl 2 rows.

Picot Bind Off: Using knitted cast on, *CO 2 sts, BO 5 sts, place rem st on LH needle; rep from * until all sts have been bound off.

FINISHING

Weave in ends. Wet block the cape, pinning out each picot, and let dry completely. Sew button on to left front to correspond with buttonhole.

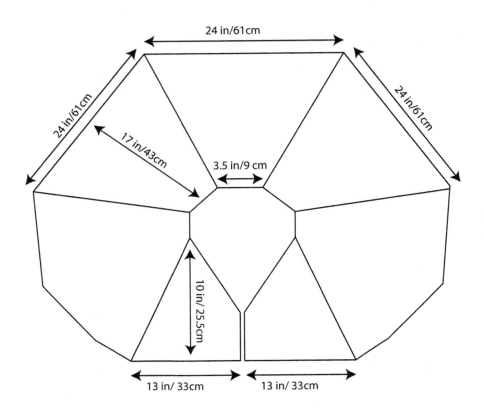

MAIN CHART (CAPE)

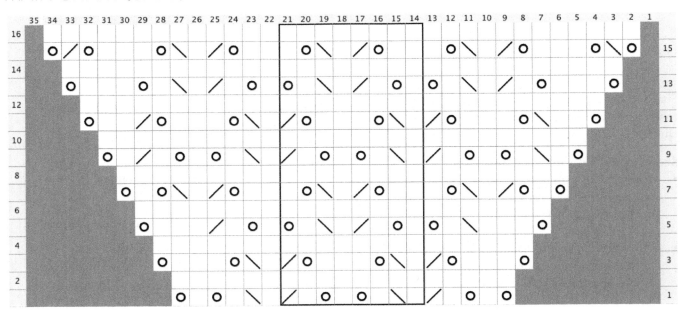

TOP FRONT CHART (CAPE)

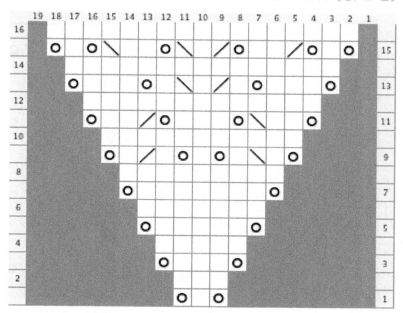

TOP MAIN CHART (CAPE)

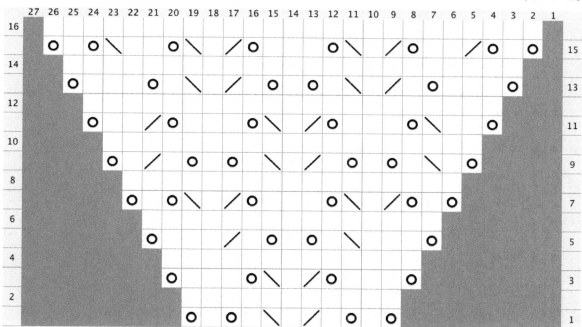

No Stitch
X RS: Placeholder – No stitch made.
WS: none defined

yo
o RS: Yarn Over
WS: Yarn Over

knit
RS: knit stitch
WS: purl stitch

k2tog
/ RS: Knit two stitches together as one stitch
WS: Purl 2 stitches together

ssk
\ RS: Slip one stitch as if to knit, Slip another stitch as if to knit. Insert left-hand needle into front of these 2 stitches and knit them together
WS: Purl two stitches together in back loops, inserting needle from the left, behind and into the backs of the 2nd & 1st stitches in that order

LEFT FRONT CHART (CAPE)

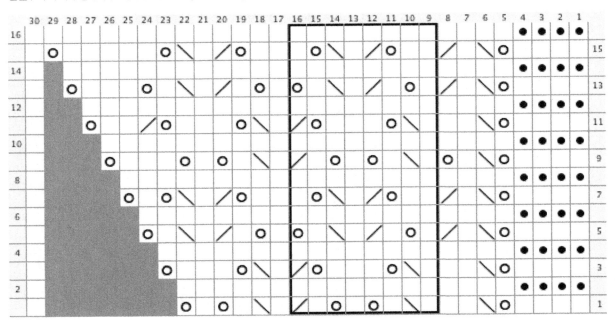

RIGHT FRONT CHART (CAPE)

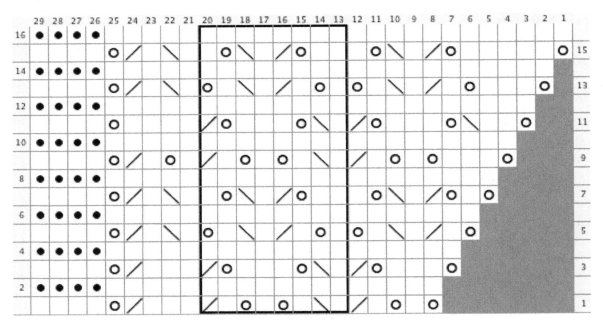

GOTHAM CITY SWEATER

SIZES

Women's XS [S, M, L, XL, 2XL, 3XL] (shown in size S)

FINISHED MEASUREMENTS

Chest: 30.5 [34, 36, 40, 43.5, 48, 52.25]" / 77.5 [86.5, 91.5, 101.5, 110.5, 122, 132.5]cm
Length (armpit to hem): 14 (15, 15.25, 15.5, 15.5, 16.25, 16.75)" / 35.5 (38, 38.5, 39, 39, 41, 42.5)cm

MATERIALS

Cascade Ultra Pima [100% cotton; 220 yds / 201m per 100g skein]; color: #3708 Regal; 3 (4, 4, 5, 6, 7, 8) skeins

24-inch US #5 / 3.75mm circular needle, or size needed to obtain gauge
1 set US #5 / 3.75mm double-point needles
16-inch US #4 / 3.5mm circular needle

8 stitch markers + 1 stitch marker in contrasting color
Waste yarn
Yarn needle

GAUGE

24 sts and 28 rows = 4" / 10cm in lace pattern

PATTERN NOTES

Sweater is started back and forth in rows to create a shaped neckline and then joined to work top down in the round.

PATTERN

YOKE

CO 62 (70, 72, 78, 86, 92, 96) sts.
Set-up Row (WS): P2 [front], pm, p1 [seam st], pm, p8 (10, 8, 10, 12, 12, 10) sts [sleeve], pm, p1 [seam st], pm, p38 (42, 48, 50, 54, 60, 68) [back], pm, p1 (seam st), pm, p8 (10, 8, 10, 12, 12, 10) sts [sleeve], pm, p1 [seam st], pm, p2 [front].

Row 1 (RS): K1, m1R, [knit to m, m1R, sl m, k1, sl m m1L] 4 times, knit to 1 st before end, m1L, k1—10 sts inc'd.
Row 2 and all WS rows: Purl.
Rep Rows 1 & 2 once more—82 (90, 92, 98, 106, 112, 116) sts.

Begin neckline shaping rows:
Row 5: [Knit to m, m1R, sl m, k1, sl m, m1L] 4 times, knit to end. Using cable CO method, CO 4 sts at end of row.
Row 6: Purl to end. CO 4 sts at end of row. 11 front sts on each side.

Row 7: [Knit to m, m1R, sl m, k1, sl m, m1L] 4 times, knit to end, CO 5 sts at end of row.
Row 8: Purl to end. CO 5 sts at end of row. 17 front sts on each side.
Row 9: [Knit to m, m1R, sl m, k1, sl m, m1L] 4 times, knit to end, CO 6 sts at end of row.
Row 10: Purl to end. CO 6 sts at end of row. 24 front sts on each side.
Row 11: [Knit to m, m1R, sl m, k1, sl m, m1L] 4 times, knit to end. At end of row, CO 1 (3, 6, 7, 9, 12, 16) sts, pm (alternate color) to indicate beg of rnd, CO 1 (3, 6, 7, 9, 12, 16) more sts and join, being careful not to twist—50 (54, 60, 62, 66, 72, 80) front/back sts, 20 (22, 20, 22, 24, 24, 22) sleeve sts.

Raglan Inc Rnds:
Rnd 1: Knit.
Rnd 2: [Knit to m, m1R, sl m, k1, sl m, m1L] 3 times, knit to end.
Rep these 2 rnds 16 (19, 20, 23, 26, 30, 31) more times. Seam sts are now added to sleeve st count—84 (94, 102, 110, 120, 134, 144) front/back sts, 56 (64, 64, 72, 80, 88, 88) sleeve sts, 280 (316, 332, 364, 400, 444, 464) total sts.

DIVIDE SLEEVES

Knit to first raglan m. Remove m. *Slip 56 (64, 64, 72, 80, 80, 88, 88) onto waste yarn, remove m, k21 (24, 26, 28, 30, 34, 36), pm, k42 (46, 50, 54, 60, 66, 72), pm*, k21 (24, 26, 28, 30, 34, 36); rep from * to * once more, pm—168 (188, 204, 220, 240, 268, 288) sts total.

Knit even for 4 (4.5, 4.75, 5.25, 6.25, 7, 7.5)" / 10 (11.5, 12, 13.5, 16, 18, 19)cm, approx 28 (32, 34, 37, 44, 53) rnds, or length required to nearly cover bust while stretching lightly.

Dec Rnd: [Work to 2 sts before m, k2tog, sl m, work to m, sl m, ssk] twice, work to end.
Rep Dec Rnd every 5 (5, 5, 3, 3, 3, 3) rnds 2 (3, 2, 6, 7, 8, 7) more times—156 (172, 192, 192, 208, 232, 256) sts.

Work even for 5.5 (5.5, 5.5, 4, 1.25, 1.25, 1.25)" / 14 (14, 14, 10, 3, 3, 3)cm, or approx 38 (38, 38, 28, 9, 9, 9) rows.

Inc Rnd: [Work to m, m1R, sl m, work to m, slm, m1L] twice.
Rep Inc Rnd every 5 (5, 5, 3, 3, 3, 3) rows 4 (4, 5, 7, 9, 11, 11) more times—176 (192, 216, 224, 248, 280, 304) sts.
Work in lace patt for 16 rnds. BO loosely.

SLEEVES

Place held 56 (64, 64, 72, 80, 88, 88) sleeve sts on the needles and distribute evenly to work in the rnd. Knit 1 rnd. Work in lace patt for 16 rnds. BO loosely.

FINISHING

Neck Edging: With RS facing and smaller needle, starting at front left side raglan seam, join yarn and pick up and knit 24 sts along left front side, 2 (6, 12, 14, 18, 24, 32) sts along front center of neckline, 24 sts from right side to front right raglan seam, 9 (11, 9, 11, 13, 13, 11) sts across right shoulder, 39 (43, 49, 51, 55, 61, 69) sts across back neck, and 9 (11, 9, 11, 13, 13, 11) sts across left shoulder—107 (119, 127, 135, 147, 159, 171) sts total. Pm, join to work in the round. Purl 1 rnd. BO loosely.

Block and weave in ends.

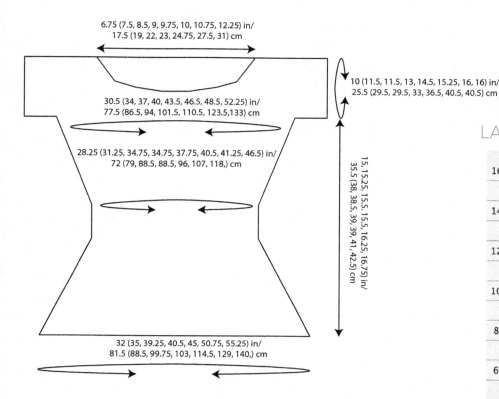

6.75 (7.5, 8.5, 9, 9.75, 10, 10.75, 12.25) in/
17.5 (19, 22, 23, 24.75, 27.5, 31) cm

10 (11.5, 11.5, 13, 14.5, 15.25, 16, 16) in/
25.5 (29.5, 29.5, 33, 36.5, 40.5, 40.5) cm

30.5 (34, 37, 40, 43.5, 46.5, 48.5, 52.25) in/
77.5 (86.5, 94, 101.5, 110.5, 123.5,133) cm

28.25 (31.25, 34.75, 34.75, 37.75, 40.5, 41.25, 46.5) in/
72 (79, 88.5, 88.5, 96, 107, 118,) cm

15, 15.25, 15.5, 15.5, 16.25, 16.75) in/
35.5 (38, 38.5, 39, 39, 41, 42.5) cm

32 (35, 39.25, 40.5, 45, 50.75, 55.25) in/
81.5 (88.5, 99.75, 103, 114.5, 129, 140,) cm

LACE CHART (SWEATER)

knit
RS: knit stitch
WS: purl stitch

ssk
RS: Slip one stitch as if to knit, Slip another stitch as if to knit. Insert left-hand needle into front of these 2 stitches and knit them together
WS: Purl two stitches together in back loops, inserting needle from the left, behind and into the backs of the 2nd & 1st stitches in that order

yo
RS: Yarn Over
WS: Yarn Over

k2tog
RS: Knit two stitches together as one stitch
WS: Purl 2 stitches together

LACE PATTERN

Rnd 1 (RS): *K1, ssk, [k1, yo] twice, k1, k2tog; rep from * to end of rnd.

Rnd 2 and all even-numbered rnds: Knit.

Rnd 3: *k1, ssk, yo, k3, yo, k2tog; rep from * to end of rnd.

Rnd 5: *K1, yo, k1, k2tog, k1, ssk, k1, yo; rep from * to end of rnd.

Rnd 7: *K2, yo, k2tog, k1, ssk, yo, k1; rep from * to end of rnd.

Rnd 9: *k1, ssk, k1, yo, k1, yo, k1, k2tog; rep from * to end of rnd.

Rnd 11:*k1, ssk, yo, k3, yo, k2tog; rep from * to end of rnd.

Rnd 13: *k1, yo, k1, k2tog, k1, ssk, k1, yo; rep from * to end of rnd.

Rnd 15: *k2, yo, k2tog, k1, ssk, yo, k1; rep from * to end of rnd.

MS. PAROO
BY MEGHAN JONES

A rguably Hollywood's most famous librarian, Marian Paroo is every bit the stereotype—a prim spinster with glasses who wears her hair in a bun. As played by Shirley Jones in the 1962 film *The Music Man*, however, she's not at all mousy: she's educated and sensible, she defends her collection from accusations of "smuttiness," and thanks to solid research skills, she sees through con-man Professor Harold Hill. Despite her spinsterish demeanor, she is a romantic at heart, and it is her clear-sightedness and compassion that save the day.

The puffed sleeves, nipped waist, and delicate buttons of Meghan Jones' cardigan are reminiscent of turn-of-the-century fashion, while the feminine stitch pattern and soft, orchid pink yarn hint at a librarian's dreamier side. Just like Marian, Ms. Paroo perfectly blends convention, romance, and style.

SIZES
Women's XS [S, M, L, XL, 2XL, 3XL] (shown in size S)

FINISHED MEASUREMENTS
Chest: 33 [37, 40.5, 44.5, 48, 52, 56]" / 84 [94, 103, 113, 122, 132, 142]cm
Length: 21.25 [21.75, 22.5, 22.5, 22.75, 23, 23.5]" / 54 [55, 57, 57, 58, 58.5, 59.5]cm

MATERIALS
Cascade Yarns Cloud 9 [50% merino, 50% angora; 109 yds / 100m per 50g skein]; color #114; 8 [9, 10, 10, 11, 12, 13] skeins

24-inch US #7 / 4.5mm circular needle, or size needed to obtain gauge

Yarn needle
Seven 7½" / 19cm diameter buttons
Stitch markers

GAUGE
19 sts and 28 rows = 4" / 10cm in St st
24 sts and 24 rows = 4" / 10cm in Smocked patt

PATTERN NOTES
Smocked Stitch changes stitch counts on Rows 2 and 6, only count stitches after working Rows 4 or 8.

During decreases and increases for side and armhole shaping only work smocked pattern at garment edge when there are 4 sts available over 4 rows not including garter selvedge stitch or decrease stitch. Do not work half a smock over 2 sts. Work any rem sts not used in smocked pattern as stockinette sts (knit on RS and purl on WS).

During Right Front, buttonholes are worked throughout the length of the front up to the neckline shaping. Read pattern throughout to ensure buttonhole placement is correct.

Buttonhole Row (worked over 6 garter sts on RS): K2, k2tog, yo, k2.

PATTERN
BACK
CO 90 (100, 108, 119, 127, 138, 148) sts.
Work 4 rows garter stitch.

Inc Row (WS): K8 (8, 7, 10, 9, 12, 12), [kfb, k4] 16 (18, 20, 21, 23, 24, 26) times, k2 (2, 1, 4, 3, 6, 6)—106 (118, 128, 140, 150, 162, 174) sts.

Set-up Row (RS): K1 (selvedge st), k2 (0, 1, 3, 0, 2, 0), work sts 1–8 of Smocked patt chart 12 (14, 15, 16, 18, 19, 21) times, work sts 1–4 of Smocked patt chart once, k2 (0, 1, 3, 0, 2, 0), k1 (selvedge st).

Continuing to work single garter stitch on either edge every row and working rem sts as purl sts on WS, work in patt until piece measures 2.5 (2.5, 2.75, 2.75, 2.75, 2.75, 2.75)" / 6.5 (6.5, 7, 7, 7, 7, 7)cm from cast-on edge, ending with a WS row.

Dec Row (RS): Work garter selvedge st, k1, ssk, work in patt to last 3 sts, k2tog, k1, work selvedge st (follow guidelines for stitch patt decs in Pattern Notes). Rep this Dec Row every 4th row 5 more times— 94 (106, 116, 128, 138, 150, 162) sts.

Work even in patt continuing Smocked patt and single garter selvedge sts until piece measures 7.75 (7.75, 8, 8, 8, 8, 8)" / 19.5 (19.5, 20.5, 20.5 20.5, 20.5, 20.5)cm from cast-on edge.

Inc Row (RS): Work garter selvedge st, k1, m1L, work in patt to last 3 sts, m1R, k1, work selvedge st.
Rep Inc Row every 6th row 2 more times—100 (112, 122, 134, 144, 156, 168) sts.

Work even in patt continuing Smocked patt and single garter selvedge sts until piece measures 13.75 (13.75, 14.25, 14.25, 14.25, 14.25, 14.5)" / 35 (35, 36, 36, 36, 36, 37)cm from cast-on edge, ending with a Row 4 or 8 of Smocked patt (a WS row).

Armhole Shaping: BO 5 (5, 6, 6, 6, 7, 7) sts at beg of foll 2 rows—90 (102, 110, 122, 132, 142, 154) sts.

Dec Row (RS): K1, ssk, work to last 3 sts in patt, k2tog, k1.

SMOCKED PATTERN CHART

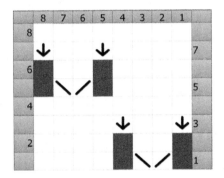

Key:

	Knit
☐	k

(RS) Knit
(WS) Purl

	k1 smock
↓	

(RS) knit into space between decreases two rows below, pull up stitch and place on right needle
(WS) knit into space between decreases two rows below, pull up stitch and place on right needle

	Knit 2 Together
╱	k2tog

(RS) Knit 2 stitches together
(WS) Purl 2 Together

	Slip Slip Knit
╲	ssk

(RS) slip, slip, knit slipped sts together
(WS) slip, slip, purl slipped sts together

	No Stitch
■	x

(RS) No Stitch
(WS) No Stitch

Work Dec Row on every RS row 3 (6, 7, 10, 12, 14, 17) more times—82 (88, 94, 100, 106, 112, 118) sts.

Work even in patt until armhole measures 6.75 (7.25, 7.5, 7.5, 7.75, 8, 8.25)" / 17 (18.5, 19, 19, 19.5, 20.5, 21)cm, ending with Row 4 or 8 (a WS row).

Neck Shaping (RS): Work 21 (22, 25, 27, 29, 31, 33) sts in patt, BO 40 (44, 44, 46, 48, 50, 52) sts, work to end in patt. 21 (22, 25, 27, 29, 31, 33) sts on each of 2 sets of sts.

Left Shoulder: Work 2 rows even in patt, continuing Smocked patt as much as possible. BO 7 (7, 8, 9, 9, 10, 11) sts at armhole edge every WS row twice. BO rem 7 (8, 9, 9, 11, 11, 11) sts on foll WS row.

Join yarn to opposite shoulder with WS facing.
Right Shoulder: Work 3 rows even in patt, continuing Smocked patt as much as possible. BO 7 (7, 8, 9, 9, 10, 11) sts at armhole edge every RS row twice. BO rem 7 (8, 9, 9, 11, 11, 11) on foll RS row.

RIGHT FRONT
CO 43 (47, 52, 55, 61, 65, 68) sts.
Work 4 rows garter stitch.

Begin buttonhole patt over 6 front garter sts starting on 5th (7th, 11th, 11th, 5th, 5th, 9th) row of work and repeating every 18 (18, 18, 18, 20, 20, 20) rows for a total of 7 buttonholes with approx 3 (3, 3, 3, 3.25, 3.25, 3.25)" / 7.5 (7.5, 7.5, 7.5, 8.5, 8.5, 8.5)cm between each hole measured from the center of the hole, while AT THE SAME TIME working shapings as follows:

Inc Row (WS): K6, pm, [k5 (4, 4, 4, 3, 3, 3), kfb] 7 (9, 10, 11, 13, 15, 16) times, k 1 (2, 2, 0, 9, 5, 4)—56 (62, 68, 72, 80, 86, 90) sts.

Set-up Row (RS): Work garter stitch to m, sl m; *sizes 42 (46, 58) only:* work sts 5–8 of Smocked patt chart; *all sizes:* work sts 1–8 of Smocked patt chart 6 (7, 7, 8, 9, 10, 10) times, k2 (0, 2, 0, 2, 0, 0), work garter selvedge st.

Continuing 6 garter sts at beg of RS row and single garter selvedge st at beg of WS row work in patt purling all rem sts on WS for 3 more rows.

Pocket Row (RS): Work garter stitch to m, sl m, work 8 sts in pattern, place next 24 sts onto a holder or waste yarn, CO 24 sts using backwards loop cast on, work to end of row in patt. Work 3 rows in patt working created 24 sts as St st.

Next Row (RS): Re-establish patt as set, introducing the new 24 sts into the patt.

Continuing 6 garter sts at beg of RS row and single garter selvedge st at beg of WS row work in patt purling all rem sts on WS until piece measures 2.5 (2.5, 2.75, 2.75, 2.75, 2.75, 2.75)" / 6.5 (6.5, 7, 7, 7, 7, 7)cm from cast-on edge, ending with a WS row.

Dec Row (RS): Work to last 3 sts in patt, k2tog, k1, work selvedge st.
Rep Dec Row 4th row 5 more times—50 (56, 62, 66, 74, 80, 84) sts.

Work even in patt continuing Smocked patt and single garter selvedge sts and 6 front button band garter sts until piece measures 7.75 (7.75, 8, 8, 8, 8, 8)" / 19.5 (19.5, 20.5, 20.5 20.5, 20.5, 20.5)cm from cast-on edge, ending with a WS row.

Inc Row (RS): Work to last 2 sts in patt, m1R, k1, work selvedge st.
Rep Inc Row every 6th row twice more—53 (59, 65, 69, 77, 83, 87) sts.

Work even in patt continuing Smocked patt and single garter selvedge sts and 6 front button band garter sts until piece measures 13.75 (13.75, 14.25, 14.25, 14.25, 14.25, 14.5)" / 35 (35, 36, 36, 36, 36, 37)cm from cast-on edge, ending with a Row 3 or 7 of Smocked patt.

Armhole Shaping (WS): BO 5 (5, 6, 6, 6, 7, 7) sts, work to end.

Dec Row (RS): Work to 3 sts in patt, k2tog, work selvedge st.
Rep Dec Row every RS row 2 (6, 6, 7, 11, 14, 17) more times.

Work even until armhole measures 5.25 (5.75, 6, 6, 6.25, 6.5, 6.75)" / 13.5 (14.5, 15, 15, 16, 16.5, 17)cm deep, while AT THE SAME TIME working neck shaping as follows:

Neck Shaping: BO 12 (14, 14, 14, 15, 15, 15) sts at beg of foll RS row, then BO 4 sts at neck edge every RS row 3 times, then BO 0 (0, 1, 2, 3, 3, 3) sts at neck edge on foll RS row—21 (22, 25, 27, 29, 31, 33) sts.

Shoulder Shaping: BO 7 (7, 8, 9, 9, 10, 11) at beg of foll 2 WS rows. BO rem sts on foll WS row.

LEFT FRONT
CO 43 (47, 52, 55, 61, 65, 68) sts.
Work 4 rows garter stitch.

Inc Row (WS): K1 (2, 2, 0, 9, 5, 4), [kfb, k5 (4, 4, 4, 3, 3, 3)] a total of 7 (9, 10, 11, 13, 15, 16) times, pm, k6—56 (62, 68, 72, 80, 86, 90) sts.

Set-up Row (RS): Work garter selvedge st, k2 (0, 2, 0, 2, 0, 0), work sts 5–8 of Smocked patt chart, work sts 1–8 of Smocked patt chart 5 (6, 6, 7, 8, 9, 9) times, work sts 1–4 of Smocked patt chart. *Sizes 42 (46, 58) only:* Work sts 5–8 of Smocked patt chart, pm, k6.

Continuing 6 garter sts at end of RS row and single garter selvedge st at end of WS row work in patt purling all rem sts on WS for 3 more rows.

Pocket Row (RS): Work garter selvedge st, work in patt to 32 sts before m, place next 24 sts onto waste yarn or holder, CO 24 sts using backwards loop cast on, work to end of row in pattern. Work 3 rows in patt working created 24 sts as St st.

Next Row (RS): Re-establish patt as set, introducing the new 24 sts into the patt.

Continuing 6 garter sts at end of RS row and single garter selvedge st at end of WS row, work in patt, purling all rem sts on WS until piece measures 2.5 (2.5, 2.75, 2.75, 2.75, 2.75, 2.75)" / 6.5 (6.5, 7, 7, 7, 7, 7)cm from cast-on edge, ending with a WS row.

Dec Row (RS): Work garter selvedge st, ssk, work in patt to end.
Rep Dec Row every 4th row 5 more times—50 (56, 62, 66, 74, 80, 84) sts.

Work even in patt continuing Smocked patt and single garter selvedge sts and 6 front button band garter sts until piece measures 7.75 (7.75, 8, 8, 8, 8, 8)" / 19.5 (19.5, 20.5, 20.5 20.5, 20.5, 20.5)cm from cast-on edge, ending with a WS row.

Inc Row (RS): Work garter selvedge st, m1L, work in patt to end.
Rep Inc Row every 6th row twice more—53 (59, 65, 69, 77, 83, 87) sts.

Work even in patt continuing Smocked patt and single garter selvedge sts and 6 front button band garter sts until piece measures 13.75 (13.75, 14.25, 14.25, 14.25, 14.25, 14.5)" / 35 (35, 36, 36, 36, 36, 37)cm from cast-on edge, ending with a Row 4 or 8 of Smocked patt (a WS row).

Armhole Shaping (RS): BO 5 (5, 6, 6, 6, 7, 7) sts, work to end.

Dec Row (RS): Work selvedge st, ssk, work to end.
Rep Dec Row every RS row 2 (6, 6, 7, 11, 14, 17) more times.

Work even until armhole measures 5.25 (5.75, 6, 6, 6.25, 6.5, 6.75)" / 13.5 (14.5, 15, 15, 16, 16.5, 17)cm deep, while AT THE SAME TIME working neck shaping as follows:

Neck Shaping: BO 12 (14, 14, 14, 15, 15, 15) sts at beg of foll WS row, then BO 4 sts at neck edge every WS row 3 times, then BO 0 (0, 1, 2, 3, 3, 3) sts at neck edge on foll WS row. 21 (22, 25, 27, 29, 31, 33) sts.

Work 2 rows even in pattern.

Shoulder Shaping: BO 7 (7, 8, 9, 9, 10, 11) at beg of foll 2 RS rows. BO rem sts on foll RS row.

Sleeves (Make 2)
CO 52 (58, 64, 68, 76, 82, 86) sts.
Work 4 rows garter stitch.

Inc Row (WS): K2 (0, 3, 0, 4, 2, 4), [kfb, k2 (3, 3, 4, 4, 5, 5)] 5 times, [kfb] 18 times, [k2 (3, 3, 4, 4, 5, 5), kfb] 5 times, k2 (0, 3, 0, 4, 2, 4)—80 (86, 92, 96, 104, 110, 114) sts.

Work even in St st with 1 garter selvedge st on either end until piece measures 2 (2, 2, 2, 2.25, 2.25, 2.5)" / 5 (5, 5, 5, 5.5, 5.5, 6.5)cm from cast-on edge, ending with a WS row.

Shaping: BO 5 (5, 6, 6, 6, 7, 7) sts at beg of foll 2 rows.
Dec Row (RS): K1, ssk, knit to last 3 sts, k2tog, k1.
Rep Dec Row every RS row 15 (14, 14, 12, 12, 12, 12) more times, purling all sts on WS.

BO 0 (3, 4, 6, 6, 6, 7) sts at beg of foll 2 rows, 0 (1, 2, 4, 5, 6, 7) sts at beg of foll 2 rows and 0 (0, 0, 0, 3, 4, 4) sts at beg of foll 2 rows. 38 sts.

Next Row (RS): K1, [k2tog] to last st, k1—20 sts.
Next Row (WS): BO all sts, working first 2 sts and last 2 sts as p2tog.

POCKET
Place reserved 24 sts for pocket onto needle.
Inc Row (RS): K1, kfb to last st, k1—46sts.

Work in St st, slipping first st of every row until piece measures 3.5" / 9cm from pickup.

Dec Row (RS): Sl1, k2tog, [k2tog, k3tog] 8 times, k2tog, k1—20 sts.

Work 4 rows in garter stitch. BO all sts loosely on WS. Cut yarn, leaving a 30" / 76cm tail and fasten off.

FINISHING
Using yarn needle, seam fronts to back at shoulders and side seams. Seam sleeves and set into armhole using removable stitch markers or straight pins to help placement. Using sewing needle and matching thread sew buttons on left front to align with buttonholes on right front.

Neck: Pick up and knit 2 out of 3 sts around neck edge. Work 4 rows of garter stitch. BO all sts loosely.

Weave in ends using yarn needle. Block lightly or steam if desired.

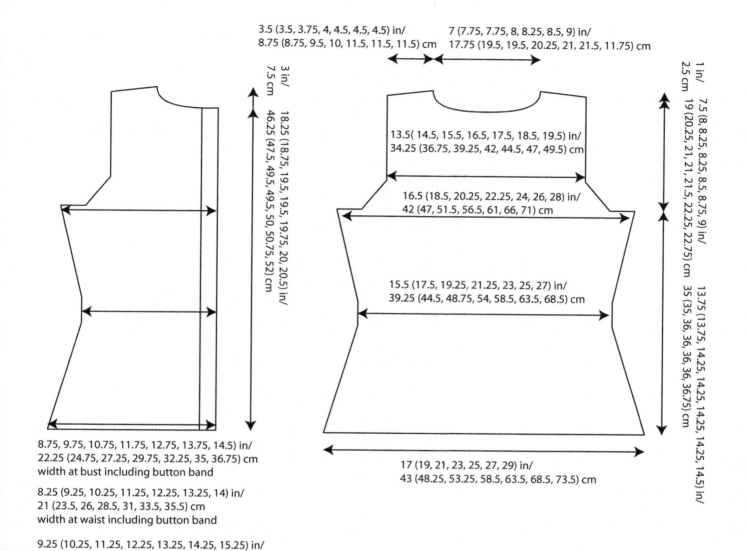

3.5 (3.5, 3.75, 4, 4.5, 4.5, 4.5) in/
8.75 (8.75, 9.5, 10, 11.5, 11.5, 11.5) cm

7 (7.75, 7.75, 8, 8.25, 8.5, 9) in/
17.75 (19.5, 19.5, 20.25, 21, 21.5, 11.75) cm

3 in/
7.5 cm

18.25 (18.75, 19.5, 19.5, 19.75, 20, 20.5) in/
46.25 (47.5, 49.5, 49.5, 50, 50.75, 52) cm

13.5(14.5, 15.5, 16.5, 17.5, 18.5, 19.5) in/
34.25 (36.75, 39.25, 42, 44.5, 47, 49.5) cm

16.5 (18.5, 20.25, 22.25, 24, 26, 28) in/
42 (47, 51.5, 56.5, 61, 66, 71) cm

15.5 (17.5, 19.25, 21.25, 23, 25, 27) in/
39.25 (44.5, 48.75, 54, 58.5, 63.5, 68.5) cm

1 in/
2.5 cm

7.5 (8, 8.25, 8.25, 8.5, 8.75, 9) in/
19 (20.25, 21, 21, 21.5, 22.25, 22.75) cm

13.75 (13.75, 14.25, 14.25, 14.25, 14.25, 14.5) in/
35 (35, 36, 36, 36, 36, 36.75) cm

8.75, 9.75, 10.75, 11.75, 12.75, 13.75, 14.5) in/
22.25 (24.75, 27.25, 29.75, 32.25, 35, 36.75) cm
width at bust including button band

8.25 (9.25, 10.25, 11.25, 12.25, 13.25, 14) in/
21 (23.5, 26, 28.5, 31, 33.5, 35.5) cm
width at waist including button band

9.25 (10.25, 11.25, 12.25, 13.25, 14.25, 15.25) in/
23.5 (26, 28.5, 31, 33.5, 36, 38.75) cm
width at bottom hem including button band

17 (19, 21, 23, 25, 27, 29) in/
43 (48.25, 53.25, 58.5, 63.5, 68.5, 73.5) cm

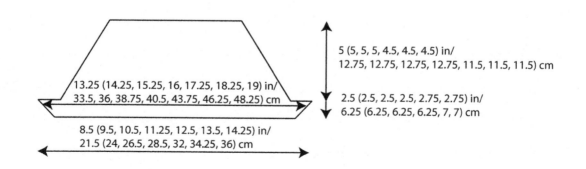

5 (5, 5, 5, 4.5, 4.5, 4.5) in/
12.75, 12.75, 12.75, 12.75, 11.5, 11.5, 11.5) cm

2.5 (2.5, 2.5, 2.5, 2.75, 2.75) in/
6.25 (6.25, 6.25, 6.25, 7, 7) cm

13.25 (14.25, 15.25, 16, 17.25, 18.25, 19) in/
33.5 (36, 38.75, 40.5, 43.75, 46.25, 48.25) cm

8.5 (9.5, 10.5, 11.25, 12.5, 13.5, 14.25) in/
21.5 (24, 26.5, 28.5, 32, 34.25, 36) cm

BUNNY WATSON VEST
KARIN WILMOTH

In the classic Tracy/Hepburn vehicle *Desk Set* (1957), Katherine Hepburn plays Bunny Watson, reference librarian extraordinaire. Bunny runs the reference department of the Federal Broadcasting Network, leading a team that provides answers swiftly and accurately on a wide range of topics to anyone else in the company. She finds herself in the middle of both a love triangle and a career crisis, longing for a deeper commitment from her slow-moving boyfriend while attracting the attention of a consultant who's been hired to build the computer that could replace her entire department.

Brainy, romantic, and a very sharp dresser, Bunny would be perfectly at home in Karin Wilmoth's crisp vest. The field of daisies over the bodice balance the tailored shaping with feminine details, while the color is a reminder of Bunny's green tulle ball gown, bought in hopes of finally being asked to this year's dance.

Will Bunny get her guy and keep her job? You probably don't need a reference specialist to tell you this gal will always come out ahead.

SIZES
Women's XS [S, M, L, XL, 2XL] (shown in size XS)

FINISHED MEASUREMENTS
Chest: 35.5 [37.5, 39.5, 41.5, 45.5, 49.5]" / 90 [95, 100, 105, 115.5, 125.5]cm
Back Length: 20 [21, 22, 23.5, 24.5, 26, 27.5]" / 50.5 [53, 55.5, 59.5, 62, 69.5]cm

MATERIALS
Three Irish Girls Wexford Merino Silk [60% silk, 40% merino wool; 240yds / 216m per 113g skein]; color: Padriag; 4 [4, 4, 5, 5, 5] skeins

24-inch US #5 / 3.75mm circular needle
24-inch US #7 / 4.5mm circular needle

¾" buttons: 5 buttons for sizes XS & S; 6 for the four larger sizes

GAUGE
20 sts and 28 rows = 4" / 10cm in St st on larger needles

PATTERN NOTES
This pattern creates facings as you go to give clean streamlined edges. Short row shaping is used in the fronts to create a stylish detail. The waistcoat is meant to hit at mid-hip.

K1 w/w & P1 w/w (aka picking up wraps):
The next time you knit/purl the wrapped stitch, knit/purl the stitch along with the wrap like this: Insert RH needle up through the wrap on the RS of the work, insert RH needle through the stitch (knitwise if you are going to knit the stitch, purlwise if you are going to purl the stitch), and knit/purl the two sts together.

Daisy Stitch (multiples of 10 + 8 sts):
The second set of Daisy rows are always offset from the one below:
Rows 1, 3, 5: Knit.
Rows 2, 4, 6: Purl.
Row 7: K2, *make Daisy (*see diagram*)—insert needle in loop 3 rows below the 2nd st on LH needle, draw up a loop, k2, draw 2nd loop through same st, k2, draw 3rd loop through same st; k6; rep from * to last 2 sts, k2.

Row 8: P2, [p2tog, p1] twice, p2tog, p5.
Rows 9, 11, 13: Knit.
Rows 10, 12, 14: Purl.
Rows 15: K7, *make Daisy, k6, rep from * across.
Row 16: P2, *p5, [p2tog, p1] twice, p2tog, rep from * across.
Rep Rows 1–16 of Daisy st, adjusting daisy placement to fit in patt.

Technical illustration courtesy of the TECHKnitter: techknitting.blogspot.com

To make buttonholes (BH): On RS row, k4, BO 3. On WS row, CO 3 when encountering the gap. Buttonholes happen every 16th row and they are worked both on body and facings. Pay close attention to set up as no other mention of buttonholes positioning will be made after they are set up.

PATTERN

BACK

Lower inner back:
Using larger needle and knitted cast on, CO 75 (77, 80, 86, 96, 105) sts.
Beg with a WS row, work 3 (3, 5, 5, 3, 3) rows of St st.

Inc Row (RS): K3, m1, knit to last 3 sts, m1, k3.
Rep Inc Row every 4th row 4 (5, 6, 6, 10, 6) more times, then every 2nd row 6 (6, 5, 5, 1, 8) times. 97 (101, 104, 110, 120, 135) sts.
Knit 1 row (turning row).

Lower outer back:
Row 1 (RS): K3, ssk, knit to last 5 sts, k2tog, k3.
Row 2: Purl.
Rep these 2 rows 4 (4, 3, 3, 0, 5) times.

Dec Row (RS): K3, ssk, knit to last 5 sts, k2tog, k3.
Rep Dec Row every 2nd row 6 (6, 5, 5, 1, 8) more times, then every 4th row 4 (5, 6, 6, 10, 6) times. 75 (77, 80, 86, 96, 105) sts.

Upper body:
Begin to work in Daisy St patt (See Pattern Notes).
Inc Row (RS): K2, m1, knit to last 2 sts, m1, k2. 77 (79, 82, 88, 98, 107) sts.

Sizes XS (M, XL, 2XL) only:
Work Inc Row every 6 (6, 6, 8)th row 7 (2, 2, 2) times. 91 (86, 102, 111) sts.

All sizes:
Rep Inc Row every 0 (4, 4, 4, 4, 6) rows 0 (8, 6, 9, 7, 7) times. 91 (95, 100, 106, 116, 125) sts.

Cont to work in Daisy St patt until work measures 12 (12, 13.25, 13.25, 14.5, 15)" / 30.5 (30.5, 33.5, 33.5, 37, 38) cm.

Armhole shaping:
Keeping patt correct, BO 5 sts at beg of foll 2 rows. 81 (85, 90, 96, 106, 115) sts.

Dec Row (RS): K2, ssk, work in patt to last 4 sts, k2tog, k2.
Rep Dec Row every RS row 5 more times. 75 (77, 80, 82, 88, 93) sts.

Work in patt as established until armhole measures 7.5 (8, 8, 8.25, 8.25, 8.75)" / 19 (20.5, 20.5, 21, 21, 22)cm.

BO 4 (3, 4, 4, 5, 5) sts at the beg of foll 2 (12, 6, 6, 6, 4) rows, then BO 3 (2, 3, 2, 2, 4) sts at the beg of foll 10 (2, 6, 6, 8, 6) rows. Sizes L & XL only: BO 3 (2) sts at the beg of foll 2 rows. 37 (37, 38, 40, 42, 45) sts.

Neck facing:
Begin working in St st. CO 2 sts at the beg of foll 2 rows, CO 4 sts at the beg of foll 2 rows, CO 3 sts at the beg of foll 2 rows, then CO 1 st at the beg of foll 2 rows. 57 (57, 58, 60, 62, 65) sts. BO all sts.

RIGHT FRONT

Using larger needle and knitted cast on, CO 46 (47, 48, 51, 61, 70) sts. Beg with a RS row, work 4 (4, 2, 4, 2, 2) rows of St st.

Lower inner front:
Note: Two different types of inc rows are used at a different rate to create shaping and buttonhole (BH) set-up is worked at the same time. If BH is to take place at the same time as any CFInc, work CFInc AFTER buttonhole has been worked. Read entire section throughout before continuing.

The following two inc rows are used in this section:
Center Front Inc Row (CFInc) (RS): K5, m1, knit to end.
Side Inc Row (SInc) (RS): Knit to last 3 sts, m1, k3.

Rep CFInc Row every 4 (4, 6, 6, 6, 6)th row 7 (7, 7, 6, 7, 7) more times AND AT THE SAME TIME rep SInc Row every 4th row 5 (5, 7, 7, 10, 8) more times then every 2nd row 4 (6, 3, 3, 1, 5) times. 64 (67, 67, 69, 81, 92) sts.

AT THE SAME TIME, make first BH on the 9th row.

Note: Before working Turning Row, make a note of how many rows were worked after the last buttonhole. After working Turning Row, work the same number of rows once, make BH and resume the 16th rep BH pattern.

Short row shaping:
Row 1 (RS): P4, knit to last 3 (3, 0, 0, 3, 0) sts, inc 1 (1, 0, 0, 1, 0) st, knit to end. 65 (68, 67, 69, 82, 92) sts.
Row 2: K16 (16, 19, 26, 31, 40), p40, w&t.
Row 3: Work in patt to 1 st before purl section, w&t.
Row 4: Work to 2 sts before wrapped st, w&t.
Row 5: As Row 4.
Row 6: As Row 3.

Work Rows 5–6 twice more.
Work Rows 4–5 twice more.
Rep Row 3 until all rem sts have been wrapped, ending with a RS row. Turn, k1, w&t.

Begin reverse shaping, working all wrapped sts as you come to them (k1w/w or p1w/w, see Pattern Notes):
Row 1: K1, k1w/w, w&t.
Row 2: K1, purl to wrapped st, p1w/w, w&t.
Row 3: P1, knit to wrapped st, k1w/w, w&t.
Work Rows 2–3 another 3 times, then Row 2 once more.

Row 11: P1, knit to wrapped st, k1w/w, k1, w&t.
Row 12: K2, purl to wrapped st, p1w/w, w&t.
Rows 13, 15, 17, 19, 21: P1, knit to wrapped st, k1w/w, k2, w&t.
Row 14: K3, purl to wrapped st, p1w/w, w&t.
Rows 16, 18: K3, purl to wrapped st, p1w/w, p1, w&t.
Rows 20, 22: K3, purl to wrapped st, p1w/w, p2, w&t.
Row 23: P3, knit to wrapped st, k1w/w, knit to end.

Turning row:
Sizes XS (S, M, L, XL): Purl to wrapped st, p1w/w, p3.
Size 2XL: P3, p2tog, purl to wrapped st, p1w/w, p2.
65 (68, 67, 69, 82, 91) sts.

Lower outer front:
Note: Two different types of dec rows are used at a different rate to create shaping. Buttonhole positioning is continued from the above section. If BH is to take place at the same time as CFDec, work CFDec 2 sts before BO for BH. Read entire section throughout before continuing.

The following two decrease rows are used in this section:
Center Front Dec Row (CFDec) (RS): K5, ssk, knit to end.
Side Dec Row (SDec) (RS): Knit to last 5 sts, k2tog, K3.

Rep CFDec Row every 6 (6, 6, 4, 6, 6)th row 2 (2, 2, 6, 1, 8, 6) times, then every 4 (4, 0, 6, 0, 2) rows 5 (4, 0, 5, 0, 0) times AND AT THE SAME TIME rep SDec Row every 2nd row 5 (5, 4, 4, 1, 6) times, then every 4th row 6 (6, 7, 8, 11, 8) times. 45 (49, 48, 49, 60, 69) sts.

Upper body:
Work 2 (6, 2, 2, 2, 2) rows in St St.
Begin working in Daisy St patt (see Pattern Notes) and at the beg of foll RS row, CO 10sts for Neck Facing. 55 (59, 58, 59, 70, 79) sts. On RS rows, work these 10 sts as follows: K9, p1, then work body. On WS rows, after working body sts, work facing sts as they appear.

Side Increase Row (SInc) (RS): Work in patt to last 3 sts, m1, k3.
Rep SInc Row every 6 (6, 6, 6, 6, 8)th row 6 (2, 2, 7, 2, 4) times then every 4 (4, 0, 0, 0, 6)th row 2 (4, 4, 6, 4, 3) times.

AT THE SAME TIME, when 28 (28, 38, 38, 38, 38) rows have been worked, begin Neck Decreases.

Note: Neck Decreases begin here and follow through armhole shaping; keep pattern correct.

Neck Decrease Row (NDec) (RS): K1, m1, k6, k2tog, p1, k3, ssk, work to end in patt.
Rep NDec Row every 4th row 8 (5, 4, 4, 3, 1) times then every 2nd row 18 (16, 16, 22, 23, 32) times.

Cont to work in Daisy St patt until work measures 12 (12, 13.25, 13.25, 14.5, 15)" / 30.5 (30.5, 33.5, 33.5, 37, 38)cm.

Armhole shaping:
Keeping patt correct, BO 5 sts at beg of foll WS row.
Dec Row (RS): Work in patt to last 4 sts, ssk, k2.
Rep Dec Row every RS row 1 (2, 3, 5, 7, 9) more times.

Keeping NDec correct, work in patt as established until armhole measures 7.5 (8, 8, 8.25, 8.25, 8.75)" / 19 (20.5, 20.5, 21, 21, 22)cm.

BO 4 (4, 4, 4, 4, 0) sts at the beg of foll 1 (1, 3, 3, 1, 3) WS rows, then BO 3 (3, 0, 0, 5, 5) sts at the eg of foll 2 (3, 0, 0, 2, 3) WS Rows. 20 (23, 23, 23, 23, 23) sts rem. BO in patt.

LEFT FRONT
Using larger needle and knitted cast on, CO 46 (47, 48, 51, 61, 70) sts. Beg with a RS row, work 4 (4, 2, 4, 2, 2) rows of St St.

Lower inner front:
Note: Two different types of inc rows are used at a different rate to create shaping and buttonhole set-up is worked at the same time. If BH is to take place at the same time as any CFInc, work CFInc AFTER buttonhole has been worked. Read entire section throughout before continuing.

The following two increase rows are used in this section:
Center Front Inc Row (CFInc) (RS): Knit to last 5 sts, m1, k5.
Side Inc Row (SInc) (RS): K3, m1, knit to end.

Rep CFInc Row every 4 (4, 6, 6, 6, 6)th row 7 (7, 7, 6, 7, 7) more times AND AT THE SAME TIME rep SInc Row every 4th row 5 (5, 7, 7, 10, 8) more times then every 2nd row 4 (6, 3, 3, 1, 5) times. 64 (67, 67, 69, 81, 92) sts.

AT THE SAME TIME, make first BH on the 9th row.

Note: Before working Turning Row, make a note of how many rows were worked after the last buttonhole. After working Turning Row, work the same number of rows once, make BH and resume the 16th rep BH pattern.

Short row shaping:

Row 1 (RS): K3 (3, 0, 0, 3, 0), inc 1 (1, 0, 0, 1, 0) st, knit to last 4 sts, p4. 65 (68, 67, 69, 82, 92) sts.

Row 2: Purl.

Row 3: K16 (16, 19, 26, 31, 40), p40, w&t.

Row 4: Work in patt to 1 st before purl section, w&t.

Row 5: Work to 2 sts before wrapped st, w&t.

Row 6: As Row 5.

Row 7: As Row 4.

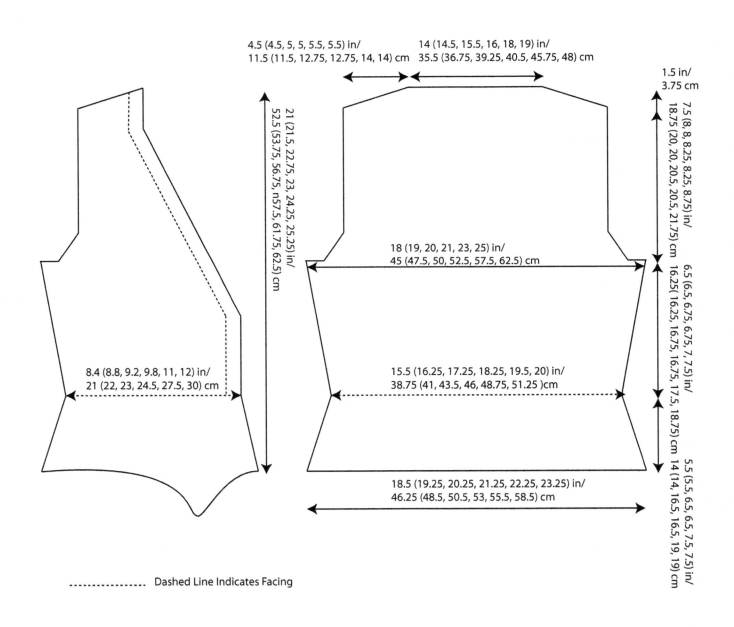

Dashed Line Indicates Facing

Work Rows 6–7 twice more.
Work Rows 5–6 twice more.
Rep Row 4 until all rem sts have been wrapped, ending with a WS row. Turn, k1, w&t.

Knit 1 row, then begin reverse shaping, working all wrapped sts as you come to them (k1w/w or p1w/w, see Pattern Notes):
Row 1: K1, k1w/w, w&t.
Row 2: K1, purl to wrapped st, p1w/w, w&t.
Row 3: P1, knit to wrapped st, k1w/w, w&t.
Work Rows 2–3 another 3 times, then Row 2 once more.

Row 11: P1, knit to wrapped st, k1w/w, k1, w&t.
Row 12: K2, purl to wrapped st, p1w/w, w&t.
Rows 13, 15, 17, 19, 21: P1, knit to wrapped st, k1w/w, k2, w&t.
Row 14: K3, purl to wrapped st, p1w/w, w&t.
Rows 16, 18: K3, purl to wrapped st, p1w/w, p1, w&t.
Rows 20, 22: K3, purl to wrapped st, p1w/w, p2, w&t.
Row 23: P3, knit to wrapped st, k1w/w, knit to end.

Turning row:
Sizes XS (S, M, L, XL): Purl to wrapped st, p1w/w, p3.
Size 2XL: P3, p2tog, purl to wrapped st, p1w/w, p2.
65 (68, 67, 69, 82, 91) sts.

Lower outer front:
Note: Two different types of dec rows are used at a different rate to create shaping. Buttonhole positioning is continued from the above section. If BH is to take place at the same time as CFDec, work CFDec 2 sts before BO for BH. Read entire section throughout before continuing.

The following two decrease rows are used in this section:
Center Front Dec Row (CFDec) (RS): Knit to last 7 sts, ssk, knit to end.
Side Dec Row (SDec) (RS): K3, k2tog, knit to end.

Rep CFDec Row every 6 (6, 6, 4, 6, 6)th row 2 (2, 6, 1, 8, 6) times, then every 4 (4, 0, 6, 0, 2) rows 5 (4, 0, 5, 0, 0) times AND AT THE SAME TIME rep SDec Row every 2nd row 5 (5, 4, 4, 1, 6) times, then every 4th row 6 (6, 7, 8, 11, 8) times. 45 (49, 48, 49, 60, 69) sts.

Upper body:
Work 2 (6, 2, 2, 2, 2) rows in St St.
Begin work in Daisy St patt (See Pattern Notes) and at the beg of foll WS row, CO 10 sts for Neck Facing. 55 (59, 58, 59, 70, 79) sts. On RS Rows, work these 10 sts as follows: work body sts, p1, k9. On WS rows, work facing sts as they appear.

Side Increase Row (SInc) (RS): K3, m1, work in patt to end.
Rep SInc Row every 6 (6, 6, 6, 6, 8)th row 6 (2, 2, 7, 2, 4) times then every 4 (4, 0, 0, 0, 6)th row 2 (4, 4, 6, 4, 3) times.

AT THE SAME TIME, when 28 (28, 38, 38, 38, 38) rows have been worked, begin Neck Decreases.

Note: Neck Decreases begin here and follow through armhole shaping, keep pattern correct.

Neck Decrease Row (NDec) (RS): Work in patt to last 15 sts, k2tog, k3, p1, ssk, k6, m1, k1.
Rep NDec Row every 4th row 8 (5, 4, 4, 3, 1) times then every 2nd row 18 (16, 16, 22, 23, 32) times.

Cont to work in Daisy St patt until work measures 12 (12, 13.25, 13.25, 14.5, 15)" / 30.5 (30.5, 33.5, 33.5, 37, 38)cm.

Armhole shaping:
BO 5 sts at beg of foll RS row.
Dec Row (RS): K2, ssk, work in patt to end.
Rep Dec Row every RS row 1 (2, 3, 5, 7, 9) more times.
Keeping NDec correct, work in patt as established until armhole measures 7.5 (8, 8, 8.25, 8.25, 8.75)" / 19 (20.5, 20.5, 21, 21, 22)cm.

BO 4 (4, 4, 4, 4, 0) sts at the beg of foll 1 (1, 3, 3, 1, 3) RS rows, then BO 3 (3, 0, 0, 5, 5) sts at the beg of foll 2 (3, 0, 0, 2, 3) RS Rows. 20 (23, 23, 23, 23, 23) sts rem. BO in patt.

FINISHING
Block all pieces to measurements.

Sew side seams together, tacking facings throughout. Sew Front facings on Fronts lining up buttonholes. Whip-stitch buttonholes together. Sew Inner and Outer Fronts together. Sew shoulders together, matching Front and Back facings. Carefully whip-stitch all facings on the inside. Sew buttons in place.

With smaller circular needle and RS facing, pick up and knit 3 sts for very 4 rows along the armhole, beg at underarm seam. Purl 2 rows, knit 1 row and BO. Leave a long tail to whip-stitch this facing to the WS of the body. Rep for opposite armhole.

Back Button Bands (buttonhole side):
CO 22 sts.
Row 1 (RS): [Sl1, k1] to end.
Row 2 (WS): Sl1, purl to end.
Row 3: [K1, sl1] to last 7 sts, k1, BO 3, k3.
Row 4: Sl1, p2, CO 3, purl to end.
Work Rows 1 & 2 once more.
BO all sts.

Back Button Band:
CO 22 sts.
Row 1 (RS): [Sl1, k1] to end.
Row 2 (WS): Sl1, purl to end.
Work Rows 1 & 2 twice more.
BO all sts.

With matching thread, sew button onto band. Center button bands at waist onto Back. Whip-stitch in place.

AURORA TEAGARDEN
BY KRISTEN HANLEY CARDOZO

The unassuming librarian-heroine of Charlaine Harris' eponymous mystery series, Aurora Teagarden is 28 years old, single, and doesn't need to look for trouble—trouble finds her. When she's not working at her local library or researching famous murders, she's tracking down—or being tracked by—psychopaths and serial killers. Either despite or because of her penchant for interesting predicaments, she never lacks for gentlemen admirers and doesn't mind a last minute run to the boutique for just the right outfit to wear on a date.

Kristen Hanley Cardozo's skirt fits Aurora to a T. Understated and simple with a ripple of lacy color running round the hem and worked in a gorgeous silk/wool blend, it's as perfect for dates as it is for shelving books or confronting criminals.

SIZES
For women's garments: XS [S, M, L, XL, 2X, 3X]
(shown in size S)

FINISHED MEASUREMENTS
Waist: 22 [26, 30, 34, 38, 42, 46]" / 56 [66, 76, 86.5, 96.5, 106.5, 117]cm
Length: 24 [24, 24, 24.5, 25, 25.5, 26]" / 61 [61, 61, 62, 63.5, 65, 66]cm

MATERIALS
Becoming Art Agave Sport [70% merino, 20% cashmere, 10% nylon; 250 yds / 229m per 114g skein]
- [MC]: Neptune; 3 [4, 4, 5, 5, 6, 6] skeins
- [CC]: Sunlit Amber; 1 [1, 1, 1, 1, 1, 1] skein

32-inch US #3 / 3.25mm circular needle, or size needed to obtain gauge
24-inch US #3 / 3.25mm circular needle
32-inch US #5 / 3.75mm circular needle

Yarn needle
1 spool of elastic cord

GAUGE
24 sts and 34 rnds = 4" / 10cm in St st on smaller needle

PATTERN NOTES
Shell Stitch:
Note: The number of sts per rep changes throughout the pattern, but it starts and ends with reps of 15 sts.
Rnd 1: Knit.
Rnds 2: [K2, p11, k2] to end of rnd.
Rnd 3: As Rnd 2.
Rnd 4: [Ssk, k11, k2tog] to end of rnd.
Rnd 5: [Ssk, k9, k2tog] to end of rnd.
Rnd 6: [Ssk, k7, k2tog] to end of rnd.

Rnd 7: *K2, [yo, k1] 5 times, yo, k2, rep from * to end of rnd.
Rnd 8: Knit.

PATTERN
EDGING
Using CC and size 5 needles, CO 255 (300, 330, 360, 405, 435, 465) sts. Join to work in the round, being careful not to twist sts.

Set-up Rnd: Knit.
Switch to MC and work 2 full reps of Shell Stitch patt.
Switch to CC and work 1 full rep of Shell Stitch patt.
Switch to MC and work 1 full rep of Shell Stitch patt.
Switch to CC and work 1 full rep of Shell Stitch patt.
Switch to MC and work 2 full reps of Shell Stitch patt.

Sizes XS, XL only:
Transition Rnd: [K5 (4), k2tog] 17 (32) times, k5 (8), [k5 (4), k2tog] 18 (33) times, k5 (7)—220 (340) sts.

Sizes S, M, L only:
Transition Rnd: [K4, k2tog] to end of rnd—250 (275, 300) sts.

Sizes 2XL, 3XL only:
Transition Rnd: K2 (1), k2tog, k2, k2tog, [k5 (4), k2tog] 19 (24) times, K1, k2tog, k2, k2tog, [k5 (4), k2tog] 20 (25) times, K1, k2tog, k2, k2tog, [k5 (4), k2tog] 20 (25) times—370 (385) sts.

BODY
All sizes:
Switch to smaller needle and knit all rnds until skirt measures 18" / 45.5cm from cast-on edge, measuring from the tip of one of the skirt points.

Sizes XS, S, M only:
Decrease Rnd: [K20 (23, 53), k2tog] to end of rnd—
210 (240, 270) sts.

All sizes:
Knit all rnds until skirt measures 21 (21, 21, 21.5, 22, 22.5,
23)" / 53.5 (53.5, 53.5, 54.5, 56, 57, 58.5)cm from cast-on
edge, still measuring from the tip of one of the skirt
points.

Size 3XL only:
Next Rnd: K2tog, knit to end of rnd—384 sts.

All sizes:
Work Decrease Rnd for appropriate size. (See below.)

Sizes XS, S, M only:
Decrease Rnd: [K1, k2tog] to end of rnd—140 (160, 180)
sts.

Sizes L, XL, 2XL, 3XL only:
Decrease Rnd: *K3 (2, 2, 5), [k1, k2tog] 24 (56, 24, 9)
times, rep from * to end of rnd—204 (228, 250, 276) sts.

All sizes:
Next Rnd: Knit to end of rnd.

WAISTBAND
Note: The waistband is worked in corrugated rib.

Transition Rnd: [K1 using MC, k1 using CC] to end of
rnd.

Rnd 1: [K1 using MC, bring CC to front of work, p1
using CC, bring CC to back of work] to end of rnd.
Rep Rnd 1 until waistband measures 2.5 (2.5, 2.5, 3, 3, 3,
3)" / 6.5 (6.5, 6.5, 7.5, 7.5, 7.5, 7.5)cm. Break MC. Using
CC, knit 1 rnd, then BO purlwise.

FINISHING
Block thoroughly and weave in all ends when skirt is dry.
The lace portion will grow more during blocking than
the rest of the skirt. Using elastic thread, measure and
cut 3 strips to 25 (29, 33, 37, 41, 45, 49)" / 63.5 (73.5, 84,
94, 104, 114.5, 124.5)cm each.

Turn skirt inside out. Using yarn needle, thread evenly
spaced elastic threads through waistband of skirt. Tie and
weave in ends. These will help maintain elasticity and
keep the skirt up. If elastic wears out, it can be replaced
every so often.

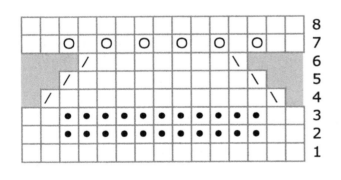

Knit

• Purl

/ K2tog

\ Ssk

O Yarn over

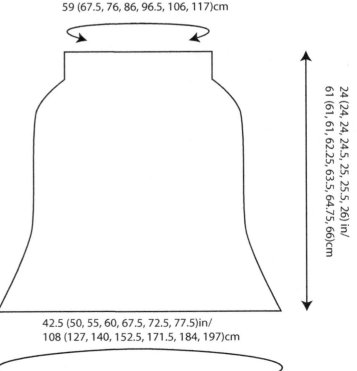

22 (26, 30, 34, 38, 42, 46)in/
59 (67.5, 76, 86, 96.5, 106, 117)cm

24 (24, 24, 24.5, 25, 25.5, 26) in/
61 (61, 61, 62.25, 63.5, 64.75, 66)cm

42.5 (50, 55, 60, 67.5, 72.5, 77.5)in/
108 (127, 140, 152.5, 171.5, 184, 197)cm

MYSTERY NOVEL COVER
BY HEATHER BROADHURST

Librarians are all about privacy. If you don't want to share your choice of reading materials, be it with your fellow patrons or with the government, they'll support you. Heather Broadhurst's clever little book jacket reinforces that privacy with the word HUSH cleverly worked with illusion knitting.

So feel free to read what you want without the need to explain or defend. After all, any librarian can tell you that not everything needs to be said aloud.

SIZE
Various to fit desired hardcover book. Samples shown fit a book measuring 8 × 5.5" / 20.5 × 14cm with a 1" / 2.5cm spine.

FINISHED MEASUREMENTS
Width: 8" / 20cm, lightly blocked
Length: 14" / 35.5cm, lightly blocked

MATERIALS
For HUSH book cover: Cascade Yarns Fixation [98.3% cotton, 1.7% elastic; 100 yds / 91m (relaxed) per 50g skein]
- [MC] #6388 (purple-blue); 2 skeins
- [CC] #5487 (light green); 1 skein

For READ book cover: Cascade Yarns Fixation [98.3% cotton, 1.7% elastic; 100 yds / 91m (relaxed) per 50g skein]
- [MC] #5487 (light green); 2 skeins
- [CC] #6388 (purple-blue); 1 skein

US #2½ / 3mm straight or circular needles, or size needed to obtain gauge

Yarn needle

GAUGE
32 sts and 56 rows = 4" / 10cm in garter stitch

PATTERN NOTES
Work a selvedge stitch by slipping the first stitch and purling the last stitch in each row. Instructions for working selvedge stitches are included in the line-by-line instructions.

If you pull up tightly on the right side when starting each right side row, you will get a neat edge but the piece will tend to pull up and in slightly. This may mean that you will need to stretch the piece horizontally to cover the book. If you are less stringent in your edge treatment less blocking will be required.

The book cover begins with a garter stitch folded flap knit in the main color (MC). After working turning rows, the cover is worked in alternating garter ridges of the contrasting color (CC) and MC before and after the illusion/shadow knitting portion of the pattern.

The illusion or shadow knitting technique is worked perpendicular to rather than parallel to the knitted rows.

The illusion word (HUSH or READ) part of the cover is worked on one side and on the spine. The word portion is worked over 43 sts; if your target book is wider than 8" / 20cm, add additional edge stitches to fit your book.

PATTERN
CO 63 sts in MC and work the folded flap in garter stitch until piece measures 1" / 2.5cm.

Establish RS and turning row.
Beg with a purl row, knit 4 rows of rev St st.
On foll row, join CC and knit 2 rows.
With MC, knit 2 rows.

Continue alternating colors every 2 rows until piece measures 1.5" / 4cm from join of CC.

ILLUSION/SHADOW KNITTING OF HUSH TEXT
On each RS row knit the appropriate color (MC or CC). On WS rows work as follows:

Row 2: With MC, sl1, k9, p3, k2, p3, k2, p3, k7, p4, k5, p4, k2, p3, k2, p3, k9, p1.
Row 4: With CC, sl1, k12, p2, k3, p2, k3, p7, k4, p5, k4, p2, k3, p2, k12, p1.
Row 6: With MC, sl1, k9, p3, k2, p3, k2, p3, k7, p3, k7, p3, k2, p3, k2, p3, k9, p1.
Row 8: With CC, sl1, k12, p2, k3, p2, k3, p7, k3, p7, k3, p2, k3, p2, k12, p1.

Row 10: With MC, sl1, k9, p3, k2, p3, k2, p3, k2, p3, k2, p3, k2, p3, k2, p3, k2, p3, k2, p3, k9, p1.

Row 12: With CC, sl1, k12, p2, k3, p2, k3, p2, k3, p2, k3, p2, k3, p2, k3, p2, k3, p2, k12, p1.

Row 14: With MC, Sl1, k9, p3, k2, p3, k2, p3, k2, p3, k2, p8, k2, p3, k2, p3, k2, p3, k9, p1.

Row 16: With CC, sl1, k12, p2, k3, p2, k3, p2, k3, p2, k8, p2, k3, p2, k3, p2, k3, p2, k12, p1.

Row 18: With MC, sl1, k9, p3, k7, p3, k2, p3, k2, p4, k6, p3, k7, p3, k9, p1.

Row 20: With CC, sl1, k12, p7, k3, p2, k3, p2, k4, p6, k3, p7, k12, p1.

Row 22: With MC, sl1, k9, p3, k7, p3, k2, p3, k2, p3, k6, p4, k7, p3, k9, p1.

Row 24: With CC, sl1, k12, p7, k3, p2, k3, p2, k3, p6, k4, p7, k3, k12, p1.

Row 26: With MC, sl1, k9, p3, k2, p3, k2, p3, k2, p3, k2, p3, k2, p8, k2, p3, k2, p3, k9, p1.

Row 28: With CC, sl1, k12, p2, k3, p2, k3, p2, k3, p2, k3, p2, k8, p2, k3, p2, k12, p1.

Row 30: With MC, sl1, k9, p3, k2, p3, k2, p3, k2, p3, k2, p3, k2, p3, k2, p3, k2, p3, k9, p1.

Row 32: With CC, sl1, k12, p2, k3, p2, k3, p2, k3, p2, k3, p2, k3, p2, k3, p2, k12, p1.

Row 34: With MC, sl1, k9, p3, k2, p3, k2, p3, k2, p3, k2, p3, k7, p3, k2, p3, k2, p3, k9, p1.

Row 36: With CC, sl1, k12, p2, k3, p2, k3, p2, k3, p2, k3, p7, k3, p2, k3, p2, k12, p1.

Row 38: With MC, sl1, k9, p3, k2, p3, k2, p3, k2, p3, k2, p4, k5, p4, k2, p3, k2, p3, k9, p1.

Row 40: With CC, sl1, k61, p1.

With MC, knit 2 rows.
With CC, knit 2 rows.
Continue alternating colors every 2 rows until piece measures 5.5" / 14cm from join of CC.

ILLUSION/SHADOW KNITTING ON SPINE

On each RS row knit the appropriate color (MC or CC). On WS rows work as follows:

Row 2: With MC, sl1, k5, p5, k5, p5, k5, p5, k1, p5, k5, p5, k5, p5, k5, p1.

Row 4: With CC, sl1, p5, k5, p5, k5, p5, k5, p1, k5, p5, k5, p5, k5, p6.

Row 6: With MC, sl1, k4, p5, k5, p5, k5, p5, k3, p5, k5, p5, k5, p5, k4, p1.

Row 8: With CC, sl1, p4, k5, p5, k5, p5, k5, p3, k5, p5, k5, p5, k5, p5.

Row 10: With MC, sl1, k3, p5, k5, p5, k5, p5, k5, p5, k5, p5, k5, p5, k3, p1.

Row 12: With CC, sl1, p3, k5, p5, k5, p5, k5, p5, k5, p5, k5, k5, p4.

Row 14: With MC, sl1, k2, p5, k5, p5, k5, p7, k5, p5, k5, p5, k5, p5, k2, p1.

Row 16: With CC, sl1, k61, p1.

Change to MC and knit 2 rows.
Change to CC and knit 2 rows.
Continue alternating colors every two rows until piece measures 12" / 30.5cm from join of CC.
Leaving a length of about 6" / 15cm, cut CC.

With MC, knit 2 rows and then establish fold line for flap as follows: Beg with a purl row, knit 4 rows of rev St st. Work in garter stitch until piece measures 14" / 35.5cm. BO loosely. Try to BO so that the MC end will be opposite the CC end. In this manner, you can use CC to tack one side of the flap and MC to tack the other.

Leaving a length of about 6" / 15cm, cut MC.
Thread MC yarn end onto a yarn needle.
Fold flap and use MC yarn to tack flap to WS of cover.
Rep using MC yarn end for other flap.

ILLUSION/SHADOW KNITTING OF READ TEXT

On each RS row knit the appropriate color (MC or CC) on WS rows work as follows:

Row 2: With MC, sl1, k9, p3, k2, p3, k2, p3, k7, p3, k2, p3, k2, p3, k5, p5, k9, p1.

Row 4: With CC, sl1, k12, p2, k3, p2, k3, p7, k3, p2, k3, p2, k3, p5, k14, p1.

Row 6: With MC, sl1, k9, p3, k2, p3, k2, p3, k7, p3, k2, p3, k2, p3, k6, p4, k9, p1.

Row 8: With CC, sl1, k12, p2, k3, p2, k3, p7, k3, p2, k3, p2, k3, p6, k13, p1.

Row 10: With MC, sl1, k9, p3, k2, p2, k2, p4, k2, p8, k2, p3, k2, p3, k2, p2, k3, p3, k9, p1.

Row 12: With CC, sl1, k12, p2, k2, p2, k4, p2, k8, p2, k3, p2, k3, p2, k2, p3, k12, p1.

Row 14: With MC, sl1, k9, p3, k2, p2, k2, p4, k2, p8, k2, p3, k2, p3, k2, p3, k2, p3, k9, p1.

Row 16: With CC, sl1, k12, p2, k2, p2, k4, p2, k8, p2, k3, p2, k3, p2, k12, p1.

Row 18: With MC, sl1, k9, p3, k5, p5, k5, k7, p3, k2, p3, k2, p3, k9, p1.

Row 20: With CC, sl1, k12, p5, k5, p5, k5, p7, k3, p2, k3, p2, k12, p1.

Row 22: With MC, sl1, k9, p3, k6, 4, k5, p5, k7, p3, k2, p3, k2, p3, k9, p1.

Row 24: With CC, sl1, k12, p6, k4, p5, k5, p7, k3, p2, k3, p2, k12, p1.

Row 26: With MC, sl1, k9, p3, k2, p3, k2, p3, k2, p8, k2, p3, k2, p3, k2, p3, k2, p3, k9, p1.

Row 28: With CC, sl1, k12, p2, k3, p2, k3, p2, k8, p2, k3, p2, k3, p2, k3, p2, k12, p1.

Row 30: With MC, sl1, k9, p3, k2, p3, k2, p3, k2, p8, k2, p3, k2, p3, k2, p2, k3, p3, k9, p1.

Row 32: With CC, sl1, k12, p2, k3, p2, k3, p2, k8, p2, k3, p2, k3, p2, k2, p3, k12, p1.

Row 34: With MC, sl1, k9, p3, k7, p3, k7, p3, k7, p3, k6, p4, k9, p1,

Row 36: With CC, sl1, k12, p7, k3, p7, k3, p7, k3, p6, k13, p1.

Row 38: With MC, sl1, k9, p3, k6, p4, k7, p4, k6, p4, k5, p5, k9, p1.

Row 40: With CC, sl1, k61, p1.

READ COVER CHART

READ SPINE CHART

Charts are worked left to right, only wrong side rows showing.

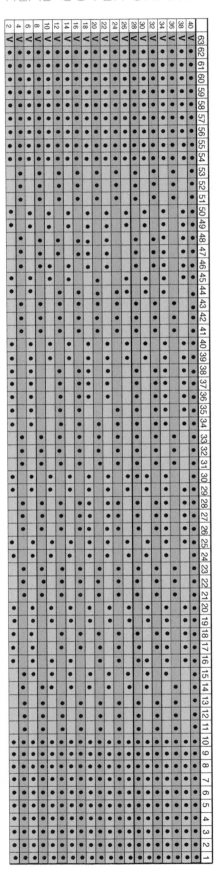

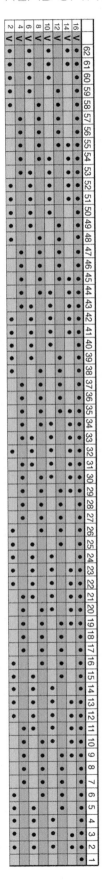

HUSH SPINE CHART

HUSH COVER CHART

Charts are worked left
to right, only wrong side
rows showing.

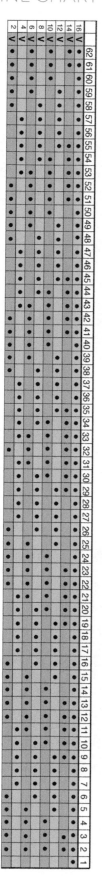

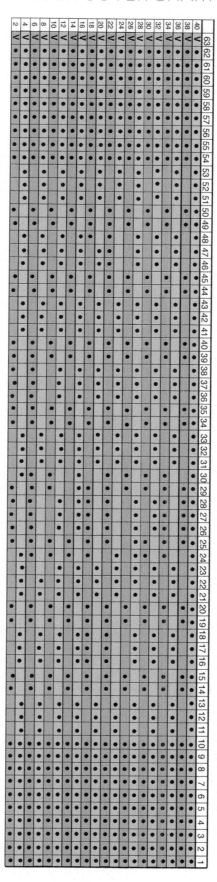

NAME OF THE ROSE VEST

I was not surprised that the mystery of the crimes should involve the library. For these men devoted to writing, the library was at once the celestial Jerusalem and an underground world on the border between terra incognita and Hades.

Mad monks and extreme censorship are the antagonists in Umberto Eco's novel set in fourteenth-century Italy. A labyrinthine library and a manuscript so subversive that someone is willing to kill for it give new meaning to the term "rare book collection." An English monk, William of Baskerville, turns detective and begins to track down the murderer using modern methods of reason and deduction. With the shadow of the Inquisition hanging over William's pursuit of the truth, The *Name of the Rose* is both a classic mystery novel and a treatise on two conflicting modes of thought.

Carol Feller has reworked the traditional monk's habit, turning it into a modern man's simply shaped vest. Its austere styling is softened with warm tweed yarn and a wide cabled border.

SIZES
Women's S [M, L, XL, 2XL] (shown in size M)

FINISHED MEASUREMENTS
Chest: 37.5 [42, 46, 50.5, 53.5]" / 95 [106.5, 117, 128, 136]cm, buttoned (2–4" / 5–10cm positive ease recommended)
Length: 27.25 [28.25, 28.75, 29.25, 30.25]" / 69 [72, 73, 74, 77]cm, not including hood

MATERIALS
Brooklyn Tweed Shelter [100% wool; 140 yds / 128m per 50g skein]; color: Soot; 9 [10, 12, 13, 15] skeins

40-inch US #7 / 4.5mm circular needle (or longer for larger sizes), or size needed to obtain gauge
1 set US #7 / 4.5mm double-point needles
• Note: You may need a second circular needle for picking up sts for front bands.

Stitch markers
Stitch holder or waste yarn
Yarn needle
11 toggle buttons approx 1¼" / 3cm long

GAUGE
19 sts and 28 rows = 4" / 10cm in St st
24-st cable panel measures 2.25" / 6cm across

PATTERN NOTES
Grafting:
Thread a yarn needle with the yarn. Hold both needles parallel to each other. It can be helpful to lay them on a table in the position they need to be worked in.

1. Pull needle through first front st as if to purl.
2. Pull needle through first back st as if to knit.
3. Pull needle through first front st as if to knit and slip st off needle. Pull needle through next front st as if to purl, but leave st on needle.
4. Pull needle through first back st as if to purl and slip st off needle. Pull needle through next back st as if to knit, but leave st on needle.

Rep steps 3 and 4 until all sts have been worked. Take care to pull yarn carefully through worked sts periodically. Make sure you do not work it too tight; it should look like a knitted stitch.

I-Cord Bind Off:
CO 3 sts at start of row, [K2, ssk, place all 3 sts back on LH needle] until all sts have been worked. Three i-cord sts rem on needle. K3tog, break yarn, and draw through final st.

Single Row Buttonhole:
1. Work to buttonhole position, sl 1 wyif, sl 1 wyib, pass first slipped st over the newly-slipped st. [Sl 1, pass the previous st over the newly-slipped st] twice, then move resulting st back onto LH needle.
2. Turn work; CO 4 sts using the cable cast-on method.
3. Turn work again; sl 1 from left to RH needle and pass the last cast-on stitch over it. Continue in patt to next buttonhole.
Note: All sts are slipped purlwise.

Three-Needle Bind Off:
With right sides of both pieces together, hold the two needles parallel in the left hand, with the WS facing you. *Insert the third needle into the first stitch on the front needle and the first stitch on the back needle. Knit these 2 sts together. Rep from * then pass the outer stitch on the RH needle over the stitch just made to bind-off. Continue from * until all sts have been bound off. Cut yarn and pull the tail through the last stitch to secure.

Wrap & Turn (w&t)
On a knit row:
- Work to last st, sl next st to RH needle, pass yarn from back to front, slip st back to LH needle.
- Turn to work purl row, passing yarn to front of work. When you work the next st, take care to pull yarn tight.
On a purl row:
- Work to last st, sl next st to RH needle, pass yarn from front to back, slip st back to LH needle.
- Turn to work knit row, passing yarn to back of work.

When you come to a wrapped stitch in subsequent rows:
- For knit sts: lift wrap onto RH needle from the front and work it tog with the stitch it wraps.
- For purl sts: lift wrap with RH needle from RS of the work and place on LH needle. Work tog with the st that was wrapped.

PATTERN
Worked flat from the bottom up in one piece. Separate at sleeves and continue in one piece to complete to hood.

BODY
With circular needle, CO 190 (210, 230, 250, 266) sts.
Work in St st for 4 rows.
Work in garter st for 4 rows.
Work in rev St st for 4 rows.

Cable Set Up Row 1 (RS): P2, work Cable Chart Row 1, p31 (36, 41, 46, 50), pm for side seam, p31 (36, 38, 42, 46), work Cable Chart Row 1, p6 (6, 12, 14, 14), work Cable Chart Row 1, p31 (36, 38, 42, 46), pm for side seam, p31 (36, 41, 46, 50), work Cable Chart Row 1, p2—206 (226, 246, 266, 282) sts.

Cable Set Up Row 2 (WS): K2, work Cable Chart Row 2, k31 (36, 41, 46, 50), sl m, k31 (36, 38, 42, 46), work Cable Chart Row 2, k6 (6, 12, 14, 14), work Cable Chart Row 2, k31 (36, 38, 42, 46), sl m, k31 (36, 41, 46, 50), work Cable Chart Row 2, k2—230 (250, 270, 290, 306) sts.

Work in patt as est until piece measures 16 (16.5, 16.5, 16.5, 17)" / 40.5 (42, 42, 42, 43)cm, allowing bottom edge to curl, ending with a WS row.

Armhole shaping
Next Row (RS): *Work to 3 (4, 4, 5, 6) sts before side seam, with new ball of yarn, BO 6 (8, 8, 10, 12) sts (remove m); rep from * once, work in patt to end of row—54 (58, 63, 67, 70) sts each front, 110 (118, 128, 136, 142) sts for back.

Note: We are now working each section with a separate ball of yarn. ';' shows division of each section.

Armhole Dec Row 1 (WS): [Work in patt to 4 sts before armhole, K2tog, k2; k2, ssk] twice, work in patt to end of row.
Armhole Dec Row 2 (RS): [Work in patt to 4 sts before armhole, ssp, p2; p2, p2tog] twice, work in patt to end of row.
Rep these 2 rows 0 (0, 0, 1, 1) more time(s) and then work Armhole Dec Row on WS only 4 (4, 6, 6, 6) times—48 (52, 55, 57, 60) sts each front, 98 (106, 112, 116, 122) sts for back.

Work even in patt until armhole measures approx 7 (7.5, 8, 8.5, 9)" / 18 (19, 20.5, 21.5, 23)cm from bind-off row.
Work even in patt until row 13 of Cable Chart is complete.

Cont to work Chart Rows 6–13 for Cables at each front, work Rows 14–21 (Cable Chart End) over the back—78 (86, 92, 96, 102) sts for back.
When central cables are complete, work these sts in rev St st.
Work even in patt until armhole measures approx 10 (10.5, 11, 11.5, 12)" / 25.5 (26.5, 28, 29, 30.5)cm from bind-off row.

SHOULDER SHAPING
We will now work shoulder shaping separately for each section.

Right front:
Working only on Right Front sts, set back sts and left front sts aside.
Short Row 1 (RS): Work to last 5 (6, 6, 6, 7) sts, w&t.
WS (& all WS Rows): Work all sts in patt.
Short Row 2 (RS): Work to last 10 (12, 12, 12, 14) sts, w&t.
Short Row 3 (RS): Work to last 15 (18, 18, 18, 21) sts, w&t.
Work to end of WS row.

Work 1 RS and 1 WS row, picking up all wraps as you pass them.

Back:
Working only on back sts, set right and left front sts aside.
Short Rows 1 & 2: Work to last 5 (6, 6, 6, 7) sts, w&t.
Short Rows 3 & 4: Work to last 10 (12, 12, 12, 14) sts, w&t.
Short Rows 5 & 6: Work to last 15 (18, 18, 18, 21) sts, w&t.
Work 1 RS and 1 WS row, picking up all wraps as you pass them.

Left front:
Working only on left front sts, set back sts and right front sts aside.
RS (& all RS Rows): Work all left front sts in patt.
Short Row 1 (WS): Work to last 5 (6, 6, 6, 7) sts, w&t.
Short Row 2 (WS): Work to last 10 (12, 12, 12, 14) sts, w&t.
Short Row 3 (WS): Work to last 15 (18, 18, 18, 21) sts, w&t.
Work to end of RS row.
Work 1 WS row, picking up wraps as you pass them.

Turn work to WS, with RS of work touching each other. Using three-needle bind off, join the first 22 (24, 24, 26, 28) right shoulder sts from front and back tog. Rep at left shoulder with last sts from front and back—26 (28, 31, 31, 32) sts each front, 34 (38, 44, 44, 46) sts.

HOOD
With RS facing, rejoin yarn at right front sts, work all 26 (28, 31, 31, 32) sts in patt, pick up and knit 4 sts from gap, p34 (38, 44, 44, 46) sts from back, pick up and knit 4 sts from gap, work 26 (28, 31, 31, 32) sts from left front in patt—94 (102, 114, 114, 118) sts.

Work in patt for 3 (5, 7, 7, 7) rows.
Hood Inc Row (RS): Work 35 (38, 43, 43, 44) sts in patt, m1p, pm, p24 (26, 28, 28, 30) sts, pm, m1p, work in patt to end of row.
Rep these 4 (6, 8, 8, 8) rows 3 (3, 2, 4, 4) more times & then work Hood Inc Row every 6th (8th, 10th, 10th, 10th) row 7 (6, 3, 4, 4) times—116 (122, 126, 132, 136) sts.

Work even in patt until hood measures approx 9.5 (10.5, 11.5, 12.5, 13)" / 24 (26.5, 29, 31.5, 33)cm from picked up sts. Work even in patt until row 13 of Cable Chart is complete. Now work Cable Chart Rows 14–21—96 (102, 106, 112, 116) sts.

When cables are complete work these sts in rev St st. Work even in patt until hood measures approx 11 (12, 13, 14, 15.5)" / 28 (30.5, 33, 35.5, 39.5)cm from picked up sts ending with a RS row.

Note: Some sizes may need to continue Rows 14–21 of cables in Short Row Hood Shaping (see below).

SHORT ROW HOOD SHAPING
Pm at center of sts.

Left Front:
Short Row 1 (WS): Work 40 (43, 45, 47, 49) sts, w&t.
Next Row (RS): Work to end of row.
Short row 2 (WS): Work 32 (35, 37, 38, 40), w&t. Work 1 RS row.
Short row 3 (WS): Work 24 (27, 29, 29, 31), w&t. Work 1 RS row.
Next Row (WS): Work to end of row, picking up wraps as you pass them.

Right Front:
Short Row 1 (RS): Work 40 (43, 45, 47, 49) sts, w&t.
Next Row (WS): Work to end of row.
Short row 2 (RS): Work 32 (35, 37, 38, 40), w&t. Work 1 WS row.
Short row 3 (RS): Work 24 (27, 29, 29, 31), w&t. Work 1 WS row.
Next Row (RS): Work 48 (51, 53, 56, 58) sts ONLY, picking up wraps as you pass them.
Divide hood at center, slide half of the sts to each end of the circular needle. Break yarn leaving long tail for grafting.
With WS facing (knit sts) thread yarn needle with yarn tail and graft top of hood working from peak to front of hood.

FINISHING
Sleeve edging: Starting at center of underarm, using dpns, pick up and knit 50 (54, 56, 60, 64) sts to top of shoulder, pick up and knit 50 (54, 56, 60, 64) sts to center of underarm, join to work in the rnd—100 (108, 112, 120, 128) sts.

BO all sts using i-cord bind off.

Front band: Starting at bottom right front (omitting bottom curled St st), with RS facing, using circular needle, pick up and knit 372 (392, 404, 420, 444) sts evenly around front of vest. Note: It may be necessary to use second circular needle for half of sts.

Knit 3 rows.

Buttonhole Row (RS): K264 (274, 286, 302, 316), *work Single Row Buttonhole, k6 (7, 7, 7, 8); rep from * 9 more times, work Single Row Buttonhole, knit to end of row.

Next Row (WS): Knit.
Work in St st for 4 rows.
BO all sts.

Weave in all loose ends using yarn needle.
Block cardigan to dimensions given on schematic.
Sew buttons in position opposite buttonholes.

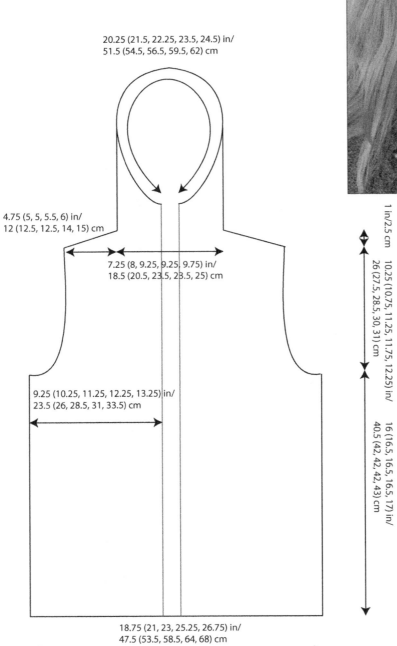

20.25 (21.5, 22.25, 23.5, 24.5) in/
51.5 (54.5, 56.5, 59.5, 62) cm

4.75 (5, 5, 5.5, 6) in/
12 (12.5, 12.5, 14, 15) cm

7.25 (8, 9.25, 9.25, 9.75) in/
18.5 (20.5, 23.5, 23.5, 25) cm

9.25 (10.25, 11.25, 12.25, 13.25) in/
23.5 (26, 28.5, 31, 33.5) cm

18.75 (21, 23, 25.25, 26.75) in/
47.5 (53.5, 58.5, 64, 68) cm

1 in/2.5 cm

10.25 (10.75, 11.25, 11.75, 12.25) in/
26 (27.5, 28.5, 30, 31) cm

16 (16.5, 16.5, 16.5, 17) in/
40.5 (42, 42, 42, 43) cm

Notes

Rows 1–5 of chart are cable set up.
Rows 6–13 are cable chart rep.
Rows 14–21 are cable chart end.

Symbol	Name	Description
✕	**No Stitch**	RS: Placeholder – No stitch made.
Ⅴ	**Central Double Inc**	RS: (k1 through back loop, k1) in one stitch, then insert left needle point behind the vertical strand that runs down between 2 sts juts made, and k1 through back loop into this strand to make 3rd stitch of group WS: (p1 tbl, p1) in 1 st, then p1 into strand between 2 sts just made.
•	**purl**	RS: purl stitch WS: knit stitch
Y	**kfb**	RS: Knit into the front and back of the stitch WS: Purl into the front and the back of the stitch
▯	**knit**	RS: knit stitch WS: purl stitch
	c3 over 3 left P	RS: sl3 to CN, hold in front. p3, k3 from CN
	c3 over 3 right P	RS: sl3 to CN, hold in back. k3 then p3 from CN
	c3 over 3 left	RS: sl3 to CN, hold in front. k3, k3
	c3 over 3 right	RS: sl3 to CN, hold in back. k3, then k3
Λ	**k4tog**	RS: Knit four stitches together
Λ	**p3tog tbl**	RS: Purl three stitches together
Λ	**p3tog**	RS: Purl three stitches together

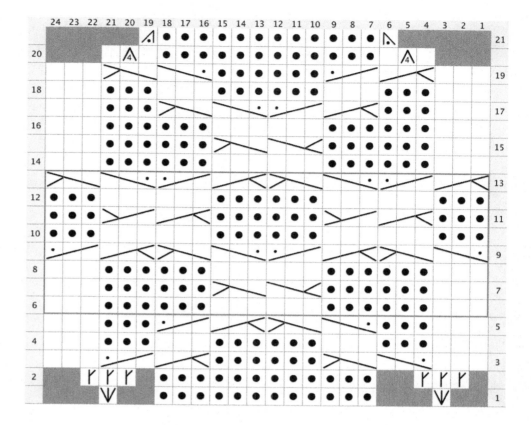

PARTY GIRL
BY HEATHER ORDOVER

The road to library school isn't always smooth, but it doesn't usually begin with a plea for bail money. In the 1996 film *Party Girl*, the fashion-conscious, hard-partying heroine Mary finds herself taking a job as a library clerk in an effort to appease her disapproving godmother—and to pay her back that bail money. Her boredom and disgust with her nerdy job are gradually overcome as she discovers a knack for helping people, learns the beauty of the Dewey Decimal system, and begins applying to graduate school—while also happening to find true love along the way.

Heather Ordover's nifty little design is a snood when worked in a drapey, inelastic yarn, and a jaunty chapeau when worked in a springy wool. Which would a fashion-plate-turned librarian like Mary wear? Both, of course (just not at the same time).

———

SIZE
One size fits most women

FINISHED MEASUREMENTS
7–9" / 18–23cm long before decreasing; final length will depend on yarn content. Slippery yarns such as Yarn Love's Elizabeth Bennet will create a longer snood. Yarn with more wool content, such as Malabrigo Sock, will create a more contained snood.

MATERIALS
Yarn Love Elizabeth Bennet [65% superwash merino, 20% bamboo, 15% silk; 195 yds / 178m per 50g skein]; color: Violet Vale; 1 skein

• Alternate yarn: Malabrigo Sock [100% superwash merino; 440 yds / 402m per 100g skein]; color: #853 Abril; 1 skein

1 set US #11 / 8mm double-point needles (if needed for decreasing)
16-inch US #11 / 8mm circular needle (or 2 circulars, or dpns, or magic loop)
16-inch US #7 / 4.5mm circular needle (or 2 circulars, or dpns, or magic loop)

15 stitch markers plus 5 unique markers

GAUGE
16 sts and 28 rows = 4" / 10cm in [k2, p2] rib

PATTERN NOTES
Written instructions for chart appear below.

PATTERN
CO 92 sts. Join into the round, being careful not to twist sts.
Rnd 1: [K2, p2] around.
Rep Rnd 1 until work measures 1.5" / 4cm.

Set-Up Rnd 1: [K2, p2] to last 2 sts, kfb twice—94 sts.
Set-Up Rnd 2: [K2, p2] to last 4 sts, kfb, k2, kfb—96 sts.
If desired, pm every 6 sts for patt reps.

From here, follow EITHER chart or written instructions below. Resume with finishing instructions below.

WRITTEN INSTRUCTIONS
Set-up Rnd 3: [K2, yo, sk2p, yo, k1, sl m] to last 4 sts; kfb, k2, kfb—96 sts.
Set-up Rnd 4: Knit.

Pattern Rounds:
Rnd 1: [K1, yo, ssk, k1, k2tog, yo, sl m] to last 6 sts; [k2tog, yo] 3 times—96 sts.
Rnd 2: Knit.
Rnd 3: [K2, yo, sk2p, yo, k1, sl m] to last 6 sts; [yo, ssk] 3 times—96 sts.
Rnd 4: Knit.
Rep Rnds 1–4 until work measures 8" / 20cm from cast-on edge (approx 7–9 full reps). Remove markers, and if desired, pm every 18 sts to indicate dec sections to last 6 sts.

Begin crown decreases:
Crown Rnd 1: [Yo, k3tog tbl, yo, k3tog, yo, k1, yo, k1, ssk, k1, yo, k1, yo, k3tog tbl, yo, k3tog] to last 6 sts; [k2tog, yo] 3 times—86 sts.
Crown Rnd 2: Knit.

Crown Rnd 3: [Yo, k3tog tbl, yo, k2tog, k1, yo, k1, ssk, k1, yo, k1, ssk, yo, k3tog] to last 6 sts; [yo, ssk] 3 times—76 sts.
Crown Rnd 4: Knit.

Crown Rnd 5: [Yo, k3tog tbl, yo, k2tog, yo, k1, ssk, k1, yo, ssk, yo, k3tog] to last 6 sts; [k2tog, yo] 3 times—66 sts.
Crown Rnd 6: Knit.

Crown Rnd 7: [Yo, k3tog tbl, yo, k2tog, yo, ssk, yo, ssk, yo, k3tog] to last 6 sts; [yo, ssk] 3 times—56 sts.
Crown Rnd 8: Knit.

Crown Rnd 9: [Ssk, yo, k2tog, k2, ssk, yo, k2tog] to last 6 sts; [k2tog, yo] 3 times—46 sts.
Crown Rnd 10: Knit.

Crown Rnd 11: [K3tog tbl, yo, ssk, k3tog] to last 6 sts; [ssk, k1] twice—24 sts.
Crown Rnd 12: Knit.

Crown Rnd 13: [Ssk, k2tog] around—12 sts.
Crown Rnd 14: Break yarn, leaving an 18" / 46cm tail. Divide rem 12 sts on two needles evenly and, using the kitchener stitch, graft the sides together to create a seamless join.

FINISHING
Weave in ends as far as possible, matching stitches as much as possible to insure tail won't pop out and surprise you.

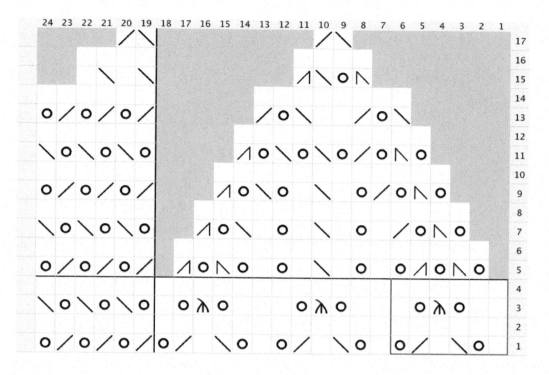

knit
knit stitch

o yo
Yarn Over

ssk
Slip one stitch as if to knit, Slip another stitch as if to knit. Insert left–hand needle into front of these 2 stitches and knit them together

k2tog
Knit two stitches together as one stitch

sk2p
slip 1, k2tog, pass slip stitch over k2tog

No Stitch
Placeholder – No stitch made.

k3tog tbl
Knit three stitches together through back loops

k3tog
Knit three stitches together as one

SECTION 3: REFERENCE

DEWEY DECIMAL HAT
BY BRENDA K. B. ANDERSON

Brenda Anderson's slouchy tweed hat has a secret code stitched into it—a number that both yarn and library enthusiasts will recognize: 746.43 is the Dewey Decimal number for knitting.

The Dewey Decimal hat features a fair isle pattern with every knitter's favorite call number and hearts (to show our love), tweedy stripes, and a cute hemmed button band. Warm and soft, it drapes nicely and knits up quickly.

SIZE
One size. Fits head circumference of 20–23" / 51–58.5cm.

FINISHED MEASUREMENTS
Circumference at button band (not including button tab overlap): 19.5" / 49.5cm
Circumference at fullest point: 26" / 66cm
Height: 8" / 20.5cm

MATERIALS
Knit Picks City Tweed DK [55% merino wool, 23% alpaca, 20% Donegal tweed; 123yd / 113m per 50g ball]
- [MC]: #25522 Obsidian, 1 ball
- [CC]: #24549 Tahitian Pearl, 1 ball

16-inch US #4 / 3.5mm circular knitting needle, or size needed to obtain gauge

Stitch marker
Yarn needle
1 button, ⅞" or 1" (2–2.5cm) in diameter (sample uses Belle Buttons by Dritz item # BB182, ⅞")

GAUGE
22 sts and 25 rows = 4" / 10cm in St st after blocking

PATTERN NOTES
The self-faced button band is knit flat The rest of the hat (from this point on) is knit in the round.

Stripes are knit using the "traveling jogless stripes" method. This means the beginning of the round shifts to the left by one stitch for every stripe. Directions are included in the instructions below.

Chart should be worked using the stranded (or fair isle) method of colorwork.

PATTERN

BUTTON BAND
With MC, CO 92 sts. Do not join. The button band is worked flat. Use a stitch marker to mark the beg of rnds.

Rows 1–6: Starting with a knit row, work in St st.
Row 7: Change to CC; knit.
Row 8: Knit.
Row 9: Change to MC; knit.
Rows 10–16: Starting with a purl row, work in St st, ending with a WS row.

Row 17 (RS): Fold work with WS tog, so that cast-on row is just behind working row. (Row 8 should be at bottom edge of hat, creating a nice fold line). With RH needle, pick up a st from the cast-on edge (make sure it is in the same column of sts as the next st), and drop it off on the LH needle. Knit both sts tog (this creates the self-hem). Rep across row, and AT THE SAME TIME, BO the 1st 4 sts of this row—88 sts. (The 4 bound-off sts create the button tab.) Do not fasten off, and do not turn. Pm to mark beg of rnd.

HAT
Rnd 1: Cont with MC. Starting with the 1st st after the 4 bound-off sts, [k1, kfb] 44 times—132 sts.
Rnd 2: Knit.
Rnd 3: Change to CC; knit.
Rnd 4: Remove m, slip the 1st st purlwise, replace m (this will shift the beg of rnds by 1 st to the left; marker still designates the beg of rnds), knit.

Rnd 5: Change to MC; knit.
Rnd 6: Rep Rnd 4.
Rnd 7: Knit.
Rnds 8–11: Rep Rnds 3–6.

Rnds 12–22: Work from chart (there are two reps of the chart around hat).
Rnds 23–25: Using MC, knit.
Rnd 26: Change to CC, [k20, k2tog] 6 times—126 sts.

Rnd 27: Remove m, slip the 1st st purlwise, replace m (this will shift the beg of rnds by 1 st to the left; marker still designates the beg of rnds), [k10, k2tog, k9] 6 times—120 sts.

Rnd 28: Change to MC, [k15, k2tog, k3] 6 times—114 sts.
Rnd 29: Remove m, slip the 1st st purlwise, replace m, [k5, k2tog, k12] 6 times—108 sts.
Rnd 30: Change to CC, [k16, k2tog] 6 times—102 sts.
Rnd 31: Remove m, slip the 1st st purlwise, replace m, [k2, k2tog, k13] 6 times—96 sts.

Rnd 32: Change to MC, [k6, k2tog, k8] 6 times—90 sts.
Rnd 33: Remove m, slip the 1st st purlwise, replace m, [k11, k2tog, k2] 6 times—84 sts.
Rnd 34: Change to CC, [k4, k2tog, k8] 6 times—78 sts.
Rnd 35: Remove m, slip the 1st st purlwise, replace m, [k2tog, k11] 6 times—72 sts.

Rnd 36: Change to MC, [k6, k2tog, k4] 6 times—66 sts.
Rnd 37: Remove m, slip the 1st st purlwise, replace m, [k8, k2tog, k1] 6 times—60 sts.
Rnd 38: Change to CC, [k3, k2tog, k5] 6 times—54 sts.
Rnd 39: Remove m, slip the 1st st purlwise, replace m, [k2tog, k7] 6 times—48 sts.

Rnd 40: Change to MC, [k5, k2tog, k1] 6 times—42 sts.
Rnd 41: Remove m, slip the 1st st purlwise, replace m, [k1, k2tog, k4] 6 times—36 sts.
Rnd 42: Change to CC, [k3, k2tog, k1] 6 times—30 sts.
Rnd 43. Remove m, slip the 1st st purlwise, replace m, [k2, k2tog, k1] 6 times—24 sts.

Rnd 44: Change to MC, [k2tog, k2] 6 times—18 sts.
Rnd 45: Remove m, slip the 1st st purlwise, replace m, [k2tog, k1] 6 times—12 sts.

Fasten off with 10" / 25.5cm tail. Using yarn needle, run yarn tail through rem 12 sts and pull tight to close top of hat. Weave in end securely.

FINISHING
Using MC and yarn needle, stitch each end of button band tube closed. Lap button tab over other end of button band. Stitch button tab in place while sewing button through both layers of button band.

Weave in all ends.

Spray block as follows: roll up a kitchen towel into a coil shape. Insert the coil into the hat and form it into a donut inside hat. Make sure that you do not stretch out the button band with the placement of the towel. Mist the main part of the hat with a spray bottle avoiding the button band. Pat the hat into the desired shape and allow to air dry.

JESSAMYN MITTS
BY JOY GERHARDT

Jessamyn West has been "putting the rarin' back in librarian since 1999." She's a tech-savvy librarian living in rural Vermont who is working to overcome the "Digital Divide," the gap between those who have access to technology and the internet and those who do not. She is also known for taking a well-publicized stand against the USA PATRIOT Act, in particular the provisions that allow warrantless searches of library records, and has weighed in passionately on topics ranging from salary inequalities to library architecture.

Jessamyn provided the inspiration for Joy Gerhardt's pretty, practical mitts. The arched stitch pattern is symbolic of "bridging" the Digital Divide; it also conceals thumb gussets and provides shaping at the wrist. The slightly challenging pattern combined with the soft eggplant colored yarn create a pair of mitts that are low-key yet high-impact—just like Jessamyn herself.

SIZES
Women's S [M, L] (shown in size M)

FINISHED MEASUREMENTS
Wear with 0.5–1" / 1.5–2.5cm of negative ease.
Wrist circumference: 4.5 [5, 5.5]" / 11.5 [12.5, 14]cm
Hand circumference: 5.5 [6.5, 7.25]" / 14 [16.5, 18.5]cm
Length: 10" / 25.5cm

MATERIALS
Debbie Bliss Andes [65% baby alpaca, 35% mulberry silk; 109 yds / 100m per 50g skein]; color: Amethyst #370021; 2 [2, 2] skeins

1 set US #4 / 3.5mm double-point needles

3 stitch markers
Yarn needle

GAUGE
25 sts and 34 rows = 4" / 10cm in St st in the round

PATTERN

GLOVES (MAKE TWO)
CO 45 (54, 63) sts loosely. Join to work in the round, being careful not to twist; pm to mark beg of rnd.

Rib Rnd 1: [K6, p3] around.
Work Rib Rnd 1 until work measures 1.5" / 4cm.
Dec Rnd 1: [K4, k2tog, p3] around—40 (48, 56) sts.

Rib Rnd 2: [K5, p3] around.
Work Rib Rnd 2 until work measures 5" / 12.5cm.
Dec Rnd 2: [Ssk, k1, k2tog, p3] around—30 (36, 42) sts.

Rib Rnd 3: [K3, p3] around.
Work Rib Rnd 3 until work measures 6" / 15cm.

Set-up Rnd: [M1p, cdd, m1p, p3] around.

Left hand only:
Remove beg-of-rnd marker, p1, k1, p1, replace beg-of-rnd marker.
Rnd 1: K9, pm, p1, k1, p1, pm, begin working Left Hand chart, stopping at the green [blue, red] border.

Right hand only:
Rnd 1: Begin working Right Hand chart, starting at the green [blue, red] border, then pm, p1, k1, p1, pm, and knit to the end of rnd.

THUMB GUSSET (BOTH HANDS)
Continue working chart as set on the top of hand and St st on palm, increasing between the markers as follows:
Rnd 2: P1, inc7, p1.
Rnds 3, 5, & 7: P1, knit to last st, p1.
Rnds 4 & 6: P1, k1, m1, knit to 2 sts before m, m1, k1, p1.
Rnds 8, 9, 10, & 11: P1, k1, p9, k1, p1.
Rnd 12: P1, m1, k1, p9, k1, m1, p1.
Rnds 13 & 14: P1, k2, p9, k2, p1. Gusset complete for size S.

Sizes M & L only:
Rnd 15: P1, m1, k2, p9, k2, m1, p1.
Rnd 16: P1, k3, p9, k3, p1. Gusset complete for size M.

Size L only:
Rnd 17: P1, m1, k3, p9, k3, m1, p1.
Rnd 18: P1, k4, p9, k4, p1.
Rnd 19: P1, m1, k4, p9, k4, m1, p1.
Rnd 20: P1, k5, p9, k5, p1. Gusset complete for size L.

All sizes:
15 (17, 21) sts between markers.

Next rnd (*right hand only*): K2, place the next 11 (13, 17) sts on hold, CO6, k2, remove m.

Next rnd (*left hand only*): K9, remove m, k2, place the next 11 (13, 17) sts on hold, CO6, k2, work to end in patt as established.

Both hands:

Continue working top of hand in patt until chart has been completed, working palm in St st—36 (42, 49) sts.

Work 5 rnds of St st.

Next rnd (*sizes S & M only*): [K3, p3] to end—36 (42, –) sts.

Next rnd (*size L only*): K2tog, k2, p3, [k3, p3] to end. – (–, 48) sts.

Work for 1" / 2.5cm in [k3, p3] rib.
BO all sts.

THUMB

Pick up the 11 (13, 17) sts that were on hold, and pick up 7 from the CO at base of thumb—18 (20, 24) sts.

Rnd 1: K0 (1, 3), ssk, p7, k2tog, knit to end.
Rnd 2: K0 (1, 3), ssk, p5, k2tog, knit to end.
Rnd 3: K0 (1, 3), ssk, p3, k2tog, knit to end.
Rnd 4: K0 (1, 3), ssk, p1, k2tog, knit to end.
Rnd 5: K0 (1, 3), m1, k3tog, m1, knit to end.

Knit 2 (2, 4) rnds.
BO all sts.

FINISHING

Weave in all ends. Block.

LEFT MITT CHART

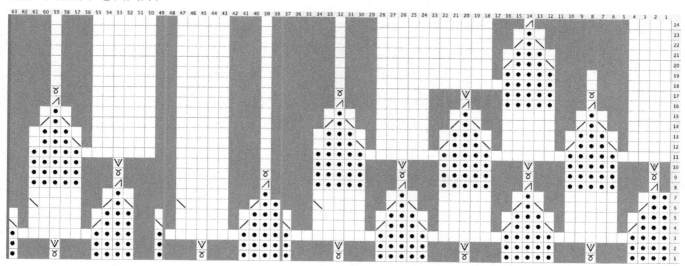

RIGHT MITT CHART

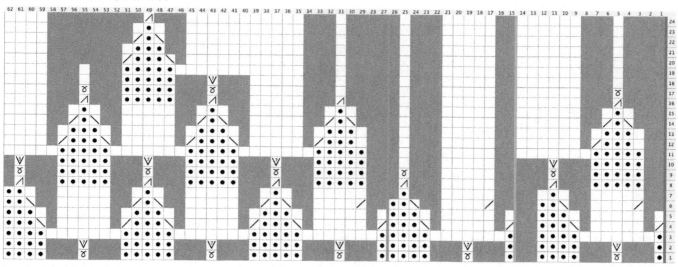

	purl purl stitch
⊠	**No Stitch** Placeholder – No stitch made.
ᄋ	**k1 elongated** knit one stitch wrapping yarn twice. Drop extra wrap from needle on next row.
�	**m7 sts in one** (k1 yo k1 yo k1 yo k1) in one stitch
	knit knit stitch
╱	**k2tog** Knit two stitches together as one stitch
╲	**ssk** Slip one stitch as if to knit, Slip another stitch as if to knit. Insert left-hand needle into front of these 2 stitches and knit them tog
⼁	**k3tog** Knit three stitches together as one
⼂	**m5 sts in one** (k1 yo k1 yo k1) in one stitch

size S: end of rnd
(left mitt); beg of
rnd (right mitt)

size M: end of rnd
(left mitt); beg of
rnd (right mitt)

size L: end of rnd
(left mitt); beg of
rnd (right mitt)

ORANGES & PEACHES SHAWL
BY THERESSA SILVER

Virtually everyone who has taken a reference class has heard some version of this story: A student comes to the reference desk at the university library and asks where he can find a book called *Oranges and Peaches*. The librarian does a quick search in the catalog but doesn't find it.

The student insists that library must have it because his professor told him it's there and he has to read it for class. The librarian asks if he knows who wrote it? The student doesn't know. The librarian asks what the book is about? The student isn't sure but insists that it's really famous—in fact, he's a little surprised the librarian has never heard of it. The exasperated but still polite librarian finally asks which class this book is for and the student tells her that it's biology.

A light bulb turns on. The librarian smiles and directs him to Charles Darwin's *Origin of Species*.

The lace pattern of Theressa Silver's spiral shawl mimics row after row of library shelves while the hand-dyed shades of peach and orange play with the reference-interview-gone-haywire. This simple design was made for a single skein of Luxe B but can easily be made larger or smaller to accommodate different amounts of yarn.

___

SIZE
One size

FINISHED MEASUREMENTS
Inner length (neck edge): 48" / 122cm
Outer length: 196.5" / 500cm
Depth at center back: 16" / 40.5cm

MATERIALS
Alpha B Yarn Luxe B [50% superwash merino, 50% silk; 437 yds / 400m per 100g skein]; color: Mango Pa-pay-pay; 2 skeins

32-inch US #6 / 4mm circular needle, or size needed to obtain gauge
• This shawl is knit flat but use a circular needle to accommodate the size and curvature.

31 stitch markers
Yarn needle

GAUGE
22 sts and 28 rows = 4" / 10cm in St st

PATTERN NOTES
The construction of this shawl makes it extremely easy to customize. The finished size, yarn weight, and stitch gauge can all be adjusted. Simply pick a yarn and needle combination that you like, start knitting, and when you've reached the desired size, bind off.

PATTERN
CO 2 sts.

Set-up Rows:
Row 1 (RS): K1, yo, pm, k1.
Row 2 (WS): P3.

Row 3: K2, yo, sl m, k1.
Row 4: P4.

Row 5: K1, yo, pm, k2, yo, sl m, k1.
Row 6: P6.

Row 7: K2, yo, sl m, ssk, yo, k1, yo, sl m, k1.
Row 8: P8.

Row 9: Each time you place a marker in this row, you will be creating a new section. K1, yo, pm, k2, yo, sl m, [* ssk, yo, k1, rep from * until 0, 1, or 2 sts rem in the section, knit to m, yo, sl m] rep for all rem sections, knit last st.

Row 10: Purl.

Row 11: K2, yo, sl m, *[ssk, yo, k1] until 0, 1, or 2 sts rem in the section, knit to m, yo, sl m, rep from * for all sections, knit last st.
Row 12: Purl.

Rep Rows 9–12 until there are 31 markers on the needle, ending with a Row 11.

BO all sts.

FINISHING
Weave in loose ends and block flat in a spiral shape.

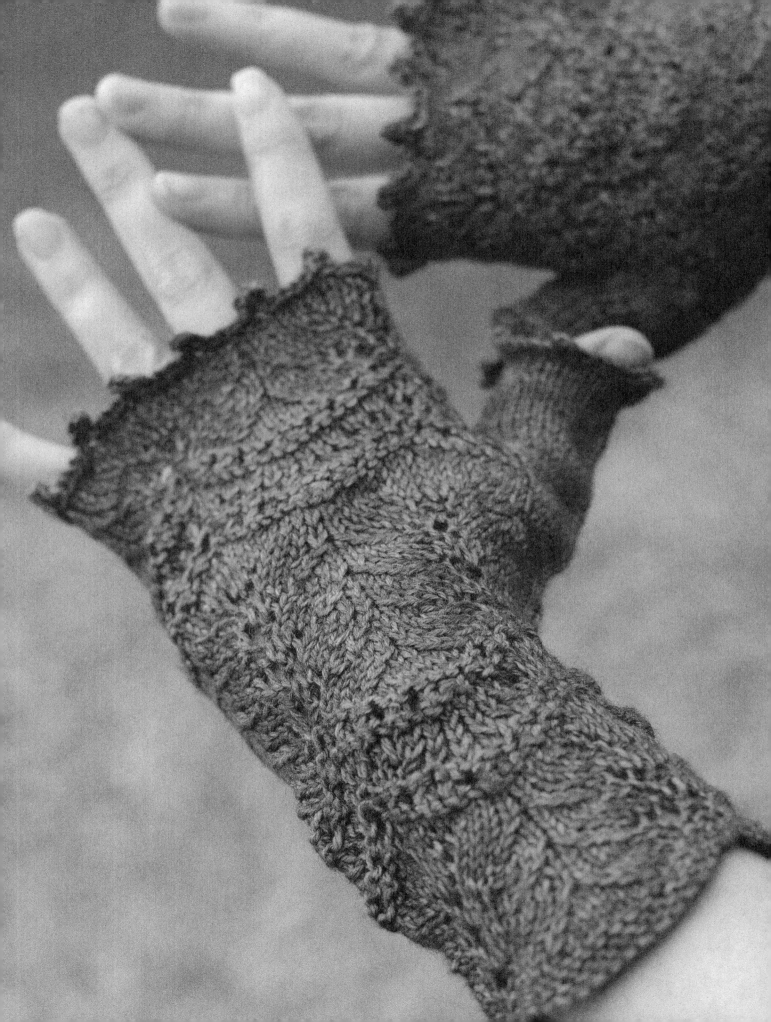

NANCY PEARL MITTS
BY BRENDA CASTIEL

Author of the best-selling *Book Lust* series, a regular commentator on NPR, host of her own local television show, and the only librarian who has had an action figure modeled after her, Nancy Pearl is a celebrity in library circles and beyond. Known for her unpretentious approach to literacy and an emphasis on reading for enjoyment, Pearl believes that one of a librarian's most important jobs is to be able to connect her readers with the right books.

Reflecting Pearl's ladylike yet unpretentious approach, Brenda Castiel's mitts are a straightforward knit. Patrons and librarians alike will appreciate the simple shape, the not-as-difficult-as-it-looks lace, and the soft, elegant yarn.

***

SIZE
One size. Mitts will stretch to fit a hand 7–8" / 18–20.5cm in circumference.

FINISHED MEASUREMENTS
Circumference: 17.5" / 19cm
Length: 8" / 20.5cm

MATERIALS
Yarn Love Elizabeth Bennet [65% superwash merino, 20% bamboo, 15% silk; 195 yds / 178m per 50g skein]; color: Art Deco; 1 skein

1 set US #1 / 2.25mm double-point needles, or 2 circulars, or one long circular if using "magic loop" method. Note: Adjust needle size if necessary to obtain correct gauge.

Stitch markers
Yarn needle
Waste yarn

GAUGE
28 sts and 32 rows = 4" / 10cm in St st

PATTERN NOTES
KLL (knit left loop): Insert LH needle into left loop of stitch two rows below last completed stitch. Knit this stitch through the back loop.

KRL (knit right loop): Insert RH needle into right loop of stitch just below next stitch; place it onto LH needle and knit it; then knit the stitch on needle.

Picot Bind Off:
BO 4 sts knitwise, [slip 1 st on RH needle back to LH needle; CO 2 st using knitted cast on method, BO 6 sts knitwise] until 4 sts or fewer rem; BO rem sts until 1 st rems on RH needle, CO 2 st, BO rem 2 sts.

Knitted Cast On:
Insert the RH needle as if to knit, knit and draw a new loop of yarn through this stitch and place the resulting loop onto the LH needle—1 st inc'd. Rep as desired.

PATTERN
CUFF
CO 55 sts. Join to work in the round, being careful not to twist the sts. Pm to note beg of rnd. For dpns, distribute sts so there are 17 on Needle 1, 17 on Needle 2, and 21 on Needle 3. For 2 circulars or magic loop, place 34 sts on one ndl, and 21 on the second.

Work in garter st in the round for 4 rnds.
Next Rnd: Establish patt by working 3 reps of chart, pm, [k1, p1] twice.
Work in chart patt as est.

At Rnd 22 of chart, work to 1 st before m, kfb, k1, p1, k1, kfb. Remove marker—57 sts.
Next rnd: Work 3 reps of chart (ending with p1), pm, p1, k1, p1, k1, p2.

At Rnd 26 of chart, work to 1 st before m, kfb, [p1, k1] twice, p1 kfb. Remove marker—59 sts.
Next rnd: Work 3 reps of chart (ending with p1), pm, [k1, p1] 3 times.

Cont in patt, working Rnds 1–5 of chart again.

THUMB GUSSET
Right mitt:
Rnd 6: Work 2 reps of lace patt, work 8 sts, pm, continue to end.

Left mitt:
Rnd 6: Work 8 sts, pm, continue to end.

Cont body of mitts in patt while increasing for thumb.

Both mitts:
Rnd 7: Work to m, k1, KLL, k1, KRL, k1, pm to indicate end of thumb, work to end—5 sts between markers. Work 2 rnds even.

Note: While working thumb gusset, rep Rows 11–14 of lace chart one additional time before working row 15.

Work incs between markers for both mitts as follows:
Rnd 1 (inc rnd): Knit to first thumb marker, k1, KLL, knit to one st before second thumb marker, KRL, k1. Work to end of rnd.
Rnds 2–3: Work even in patt.
Rep Rnds 1–3 until you have 19 sts between markers; ending on rnd 3 of thumb gusset. Place 19 thumb sts on waste yarn.

Cont working lace patt as est.
Work to thumb gusset. CO 5 sts, Work to end of rnd.
Next rnd: Work to cast-on sts. Work 1 st, k2tog, work to end.

UPPER HAND
Next rnd: Work to cast-on sts, [k2tog] twice, work to 1 st before m, p2tog, [p1, k1] twice, p2tog.
Next rnd: Work to cast-on sts, [k2tog] twice, work to end.

You should now have the correct number of sts on the needles i.e. for dpns, 17 sts on Needle 1, and 17 on Needle 2, and 23 on Needle 3; for 2 circulars or magic loop, 34 sts on one needle, and 23 on the second.

Next 2 rnds: Work in patt as est.
Next rnd: Work to 1 st before m, p2tog, [k1, p1] twice, p2tog—55 sts.

Next 5 rnds: Work in patt as est.
Next rnd: Knit.
Next rnd: [K8, k2tog] 5 times, knit to end—50 sts.
Next rnd: Knit.

BO all sts using Picot Bind Off.

THUMB
Carefully remove waste yarn and transfer thumb sts to needles. Attach yarn on right side of thumb gusset and knit the 19 sts. Pick up and k3 sts in the cast-on row—22 sts.

Knit 6 rnds in St st.
Next rnd: [K5, k2tog] 3 times, knit to end—19 sts.
Knit 4 rnds in St st.

BO all sts using Picot Bind Off.

FINISHING
Weave in all ends. Block.

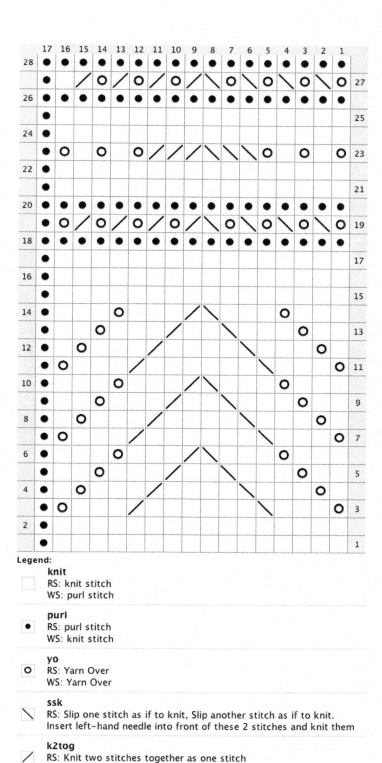

Legend:

knit
RS: knit stitch
WS: purl stitch

● **purl**
RS: purl stitch
WS: knit stitch

O **yo**
RS: Yarn Over
WS: Yarn Over

\ **ssk**
RS: Slip one stitch as if to knit, Slip another stitch as if to knit.
Insert left-hand needle into front of these 2 stitches and knit them

/ **k2tog**
RS: Knit two stitches together as one stitch
WS: Purl 2 stitches together

METADATA
BY ALEX TINSLEY

Even librarians must brave the cold now and then. Why not do it in a scarf that subtly represents both craft and career? Designer Alex Tinsley has taken the Dewey Decimal call number for knitting books, 746.43, and turned it into a unisex fashion statement. Each set of stripes represents a numeral: 7 red stripes, 4 green, 6 blue, and so forth. Dewey can be worked either flat or as a long infinity loop, depending on the wearer's sensibilities.

Ambitious knitters might want to make a statement of their own using a different classification number. For a full set, see en.wikipedia.org/wiki/List_of_Dewey_Decimal_classes.

SIZE
One size

FINISHED MEASUREMENTS
Cowl: 3.25 wide × 35" around / 8.5 × 89cm
Scarf: 4.5 wide × 81" long / 11.5 × 205.5cm

MATERIALS
Cowl version:
Blue Moon Fiber Arts Socks That Rock Lightweight [100% merino; 360 yds / 329m per 127g skein]
- [Color A] Copperline; 1 skein
- [Color B] Spinel; 1 skein
- [Color C] Pond Scum; 1 skein

40- or 47-inch US #6 / 4mm circular needle, or size needed to obtain gauge

1 stitch marker

Scarf version:
Blue Moon Fiber Arts Socks That Rock Heavyweight [100% merino; 350 yds / 320m per 198g skein]
- [Color A] Motley Hue; 1 skein
- [Color B] Deep Unrelenting Gray; 1 skein
- [Color C] Spinel; 1 skein

40- or 47-inch US #8 / 5mm circular needle, or size needed to obtain gauge

3 stitch markers, one distinct from the others

GAUGE
Finer yarn/cowl: 24 sts and 32 rows = 4" / 10cm in Honeycomb Stitch patt

Thicker yarn/scarf: 19 sts and 26 rows = 4" / 10cm in Honeycomb Stitch patt

PATTERN NOTES
Honeycomb Stitch Pattern:
Rnd 1: Knit.
Rnd 2: [Sl 1 wyif, p1] around.
Rnd 3: Knit.
Rnd 4: [P1, sl 1 wyif] around.

PATTERN

COWL
CO 350 sts in Color A. Pm and join in the round, taking care not to twist sts.

Work 7 rows Honeycomb patt in Color A.
Work 4 rows Honeycomb in Color B.
Work 6 rows Honeycomb in Color C.

Decimal Point Row: [k1 A, k1 C] around.

Work 4 rows Honeycomb in Color A.
Work 3 rows Honeycomb in Color B.
Work 2 rows Honeycomb in Color C.

Rep stripe sequence once more, and BO in Color C.

SCARF
CO 350 sts in Color A. Join in the round and place "distinct" marker as round marker.

With Color A, k10, pm, knit until 10 sts are left, pm, knit to end of rnd. From now on, knit the 10 sts at the beg and end of the rnd, instead of working them in patt.

Work 6 more rows of Color A in Honeycomb Pattern (counting the row you just did as the first knit row of the patt, and excepting the 10 sts at the beg and 10 at the end).

Work 4 rows Honeycomb in Color B.
Work 6 rows Honeycomb in Color C.

Decimal Point Row: [k1 A, k1 C] around.

Work 4 rows Honeycomb in Color A.
Work 3 rows Honeycomb in Color B.
Work 2 rows Honeycomb in Color C.

Rep entire sequence again (starting with 7 rows of Color A).

With Color C, knit the 10 sts before the m. BO all sts until you get to the next m. Knit last 10 sts. Pull the needle out, leaving live sts, and tug on them until they drop and form a large ladder. Cut the ladder down the middle to create fringe. Tie the fringe in bundles every few strands to keep from unraveling.

FINISHING

For both cowl and scarf: Weave in loose ends, block gently, and enjoy!

SECTION 4:
STACKS

OLD REED
BY THERESSA SILVER

In this classic pleated skirt, Theressa Silver attempts to capture the spirit of her alma mater's library in all its Gothic glory. The red and beige colors reflect the library's brick and stone exterior. The cables on the yoke evoke the arches and tall windows found throughout the building, while the cables at the hem represent the twining ivy vines.

The kicky little skirt itself is as enjoyable to make as it is to wear. The crisp pleats and curving cables ensure a project that is interesting without being overly complicated. The skirt is designed to hit just above the knee but the length can be easily altered and the knitter can decide whether to continue the row of buttons down the skirt from the yoke closure or use a kilt pin instead to keep the lower section closed. Either way, the look is preppy, collegiate, and fun.

SIZES
XS [S, M, L, XL, 2XL] (shown in size S)

FINISHED MEASUREMENTS
Waist: 21 [25, 29, 33, 37, 41]" / 53.5 [63.5, 73.5, 84, 94, 104] cm

Fits Hips 31 [35, 39, 43, 47, 51]" / 79 [89, 99, 109, 119.5, 129.5]cm

Length: 20 [20.75, 21.5, 22.25, 23, 23.75]" / 51 [52.5, 54.5, 56.5, 58.5, 60.5]cm

MATERIALS
Rowan Tweed [100% wool; 129 yds / 118m per 50g skein]
- [MC] Bainbridge; 5 [5, 5, 6, 6, 7] skeins
- [CC] Arncliffe; 4 [4, 5, 6, 6, 7] skeins

US #6 / 4mm needles, or size needed to obtain gauge

Stitch holders
Cable needle
Yarn needle

GAUGE
20 sts and 28 rows = 4" / 10cm in St st

PATTERN NOTES
The yoke is knit from the waist down and finished with an i-cord bind off. The lower section of the skirt is knit sideways. The pleats are formed when the lower skirt is sewn to the yoke. Turning rows are included to ensure neat, crisp pleats.

PATTERN
YOKE
With MC, CO 118 (139, 160, 181, 202, 223) sts.

Two different sets of markers will be placed in the first row. Markers designated "mA" mark the sts that will be used in the cable chart. Markers designated "mB" mark where to make incs.

Row 1 (WS): K1, p1, k1, p1, k1, p1, k3, pmA, p2, k2, p2, k4, p2, k2, p2, pmA, [k2, pmB, k3, pmA, p2, k2, p2, k4, p2, k2, p2, pmA] to last 9 sts, k3, p1, k1, p1, k1, p1, k1.

Row 2 (RS): K1, p1, k1, p1, k1, p1, p3, k2, p2, k2, p4, k2, p2, k2, [purl to mA (slipping mB), k2, p2, k2, p4, k2, p2, k2] to last 9 sts, p3, p1, k1, p1, k1, p1, k1.

Row 3: K1, p1, k1, p1, k1, p1, k3, p2, k2, p2, k4, p2, k2, p2, [knit to mA (slipping mB), p2, k2, p2, k4, p2, k2, p2] to last 9 sts, k3, p1, k1, p1, k1, p1, k1.

Rep Rows 2 & 3, increasing at the "B" markers every 4th (6th, 7th, 8th, 10th, 13th) row starting in row 4 (6, 7, 8, 10, 13) for 40 (44, 46, 48, 52, 54) rows, and AT THE SAME TIME, work a 2-st buttonhole at the beg of every 8th row, beg with Row 3—40 (35, 36, 42, 40, 36) sts inc'd and 4 (5, 5, 5, 6, 6) buttonholes made.

Beg working Yoke Cable Chart between "A" markers, working the chart once while continuing to inc and create buttonholes as described above—166 (184, 208, 230, 250, 268) sts total and 6 (6, 6, 7, 7, 7) buttonholes total.

Work 1 RS row in patt.

BO all sts using an i-cord bind off as follows:
CO 3 sts onto the LH needle.
Step 1: K2, k2tog.
Step 2: Transfer the 3 sts from the RH back to the LH needle so that the working yarn is attached to the 3rd st from the tip of the needle. Bring the working yarn across the back of the work. Rep steps 1 and 2 until all the yoke sts have been worked. BO rem 3 sts.

YOKE CABLE CHART

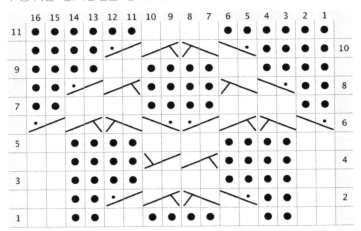

PLEAT CABLE CHART

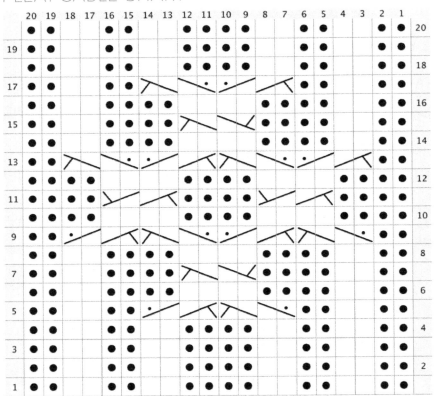

	purl RS: purl stitch WS: knit stitch

	knit RS: knit stitch WS: purl stitch

	c2 over 2 left P RS: sl 2 to CN, hold in front. p2, k2 from CN

	c2 over 2 right P RS: sl2 to CN, hold in back. k2, p2 from CN WS: none defined

	c2 over 2 left RS: sl 2 to CN, hold in front. k2, k2 from CN WS: none defined

	c2 over 2 right RS: sl2 to CN, hold in back. k2, k2 from CN

Lower Skirt
With MC, CO 71 (71, 73, 73, 75, 75) sts.
Work seed st for 8 rows.

Pleat unit:
Row 1 (RS): K45 (45, 47, 47, 49, 49), work row 1 of pleat cable chart, p1, k1, p1, k1, p1, k1.
Row 2 (WS): K1, p1, k1, p1, k1, p1, work row 2 of pleat cable chart, p45 (45, 47, 47, 49, 49).
Continue in patt until you have worked all 20 rows of the pleat cable chart.

Row 21: Purl.
Switch to CC.

Row 22: K1, p1, k1, p1, k1, p1, p65 (65, 67, 67, 69, 69).
Row 23: K65 (65, 67, 67, 69, 69), p1, k1, p1, k1, p1, k1.
Rep rows 22 & 23 until you have worked 38 rows total in CC.

Switch to MC.

Row 60: K1, p1, k1, p1, k1, p1, p65 (65, 67, 67, 69, 69).
Rep Rows 1–60 until you have made 10 (11, 13, 15, 16, 17) pleat units.

Rep Rows 1–20 once more.
Work seed st for 8 rows.

BO all sts.

FINISHING

Block the yoke flat being sure to measure the waist edge and hip edge to get the correct flair. Fold the pleats of the lower skirt when blocking; press firmly on the folds to create crisp pleats. Allow to dry completely.

Sew the lower skirt to the yoke so that the i-cord lies on top of the seam. Sew on the buttons to line up with the buttonholes in the yoke.

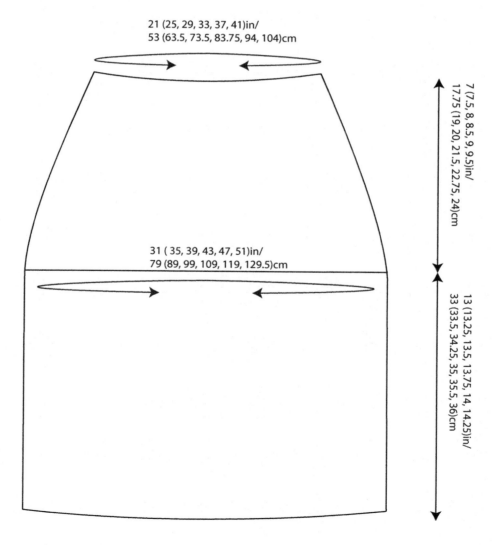

21 (25, 29, 33, 37, 41)in/
53 (63.5, 73.5, 83.75, 94, 104)cm

31 (35, 39, 43, 47, 51)in/
79 (89, 99, 109, 119, 129.5)cm

7 (7.5, 8, 8.5, 9, 9.5)in/
17.75 (19, 20, 21.5, 22.75, 24)cm

13 (13.25, 13.5, 13.75, 14, 14.25)in/
33 (33.5, 34.25, 35, 35.5, 36)cm

OPEN BOOK CARDIGAN

KRISTEN TENDYKE

Every librarian needs a cardigan (who doesn't?). Kristen TenDyke's Open Book Cardigan steps in, dressing up the librarian standby with long, flattering lines and ladylike picot edgings. The upside-down V-stitch pattern is reminiscent of a book placed open on the counter (perhaps the reader was interrupted by a patron who needed help?). The body is worked in one piece without shaping to the armholes and the sleeve stitches are picked up and knit down. Not only is there very little seaming, but the lengths of both body and sleeve can easily be adjusted to suit your height and style.

SIZES

See below (shown in second size).
Sweater is intended to be worn with 1–2" / 2.5–5cm of negative ease.

FINISHED MEASUREMENTS

Bust: 29.75 [34.75, 39.75, 44.75, 49.75, 54.75]" / 75.5 [88.5, 101, 113.5, 126.5, 139]cm
Length: See schematic.

MATERIALS

St. Denis Nordique [100% American wool; 150 yds / 137m per 50g ball]; color: #5888 Butterscotch; 10 [11, 12, 13, 14, 15] balls

32-inch US #7 / 4.5mm circular needle, or size needed to obtain gauge
1 set US #7 / 4.5mm double-point needles
US #G / 4mm crochet hook

Stitch holders or waste yarn
Removable stitch markers

GAUGE

30 sts = 5" / 12.5cm and 26 rows = 4" / 10cm in Open Book Patt with larger needle

19 sts and 26 rows = 4" / 10cm in St st with larger needle

PATTERN NOTES

Sl2-k1-p2sso: Slip 2 sts together knitwise to the RH needle, k1, pass 2 slipped sts over knit st (2 sts dec'd)

Backward Loop Cast On Method:
*Wrap yarn around left thumb from front to back and secure in palm with other fingers. Insert needle upwards through strand on thumb. Slip loop from thumb onto RH needle, pulling yarn to tighten. Rep from * for desired number of sts.

4-Stitch One-Row Buttonhole:
With RS facing, bring yarn to front, sl 1 st purlwise, return yarn to the back, *sl 1 st purlwise, pass the first slipped st over the second slipped st as if to BO; rep from * 3 more times. Slip the st on the RH needle back to the LH needle and turn so WS is facing. **With yarn in back, insert RH needle between the first 2 sts on the LH needle, draw through a loop and place it on the LH needle; rep from ** 4 more times then turn so RS is facing. With yarn in back, sl 1 st from LH needle to RH needle and pass the last CO st over that st to close the buttonhole.

2 × 2 Ribbing (multiple of 4 sts):
All rnds: [K1, p2, k1] around.

Wrap and turn:
- Knit row: Wyib, slip next st purlwise onto RH needle, bring yarn to front of work, return slipped st to LH needle, bring yarn to back of work, then turn work.
- Purl row: Wyif slip next st purlwise onto RH needle, bring yarn to back of work, return slipped st to LH needle, bring yarn to front of work, then turn work.

Hide wraps:
- Knit row: Pick up the wrap from the front with the RH needle and knit together with the st it wraps.
- Purl row: Pick up the wrap through back of loop with RH needle and purl together with the st it wraps.

Circular needle is used to accommodate large number of sts. Do not join; work back and forth in rows.

Lower edge of body will flare out a bit. If less flare is desired, CO fewer sts, then increase to the indicated number of sts after the joining row.

PATTERN

BODY

With larger circular needle, CO 193 (223, 253, 283, 313, 343) sts. Beg with a WS row, work in St st for 17 rows, ending after a WS row.

Turning Row: (RS) K1, *yo, k2tog; rep from * to end. Cont in St st for 17 rows, ending after a WS row.

Joining Row: (RS) Use the backwards loop method to CO 12 sts for right front band facing, k25, fold work to the WS along turning row, *with LH needle, pick up the CO st that aligns with the next st on the LH needle, knit those 2 sts together, k1; rep from * to last 12 sts, knit to end, use the backwards loop method to CO 13 sts for left front band facing. 217 (247, 277, 307, 337, 367) sts.

Next Row: (WS) P25, knit to last 25 sts, purl to end.

Est Patt: Work 12 sts in St st, sl 1 purlwise wyib for turning st, work 12 sts in St st, work in Open Book Patt to last 25 sts, work 12 sts in St st, sl 1 purlwise wyib for turning st, work 12 sts in St st. Cont working as est until piece meas 15.75" / 40cm from turning row, purling into the slipped sts on each WS row, and ending after a WS row.

Note: Read the foll instructions carefully before cont, the armholes are divided before the buttonholes are completed.

Buttonhole Row: (RS) Work 4 sts, work 4-st buttonhole, work 7 sts as est, work 4-st buttonhole, work to end as est. *Work even for 2.75" / 7cm, ending after a WS row, then rep buttonhole row; rep from * once more; and at the same time, when piece meas 19" / 48.5cm from turning row, end after a WS row.

OPEN BOOK PATTERN

	17	16	15	14	13	12	11	10	9	8	7	6	5	4	3	2	1	
6	●	●							●							●	●	
	●	●	MR						⟋•						ML	●	●	5
4	●	●						●	●	●						●	●	
	●	●	MR					●	⟋•	●					ML	●	●	3
2	●	●					●	●	●	●	●					●	●	
	●	●	MR				●	●	⟋•	●	●				ML	●	●	1

Legend:

● **purl**
RS: purl stitch
WS: knit stitch

M **make one left**
RS: Place a firm backward loop over the right needle, so that the yarn end goes towards the front
WS: Place a firm backward loop over the right needle, so that the yarn end goes towards the back

(blank) **knit**
RS: knit stitch
WS: purl stitch

⟋• **p3tog**
RS: Purl three stitches together as one
WS: Knit three stitches together as one

MR **make one right**
RS: Place a firm backward loop over the right needle, so that the yarn end goes towards the back
WS: Place a firm backward loop over the right needle, so that the yarn end goes towards the front

WRITTEN INSTRUCTIONS
(mulitiple of 15 sts + 2)

Row 1: (RS) P2, *m1L, k3, p2, p3tog, p2, k3, m1R, p2; rep from *.

Row 2: K2, *p4, k5, p4, k2; rep from *.

Row 3: P2, *m1L, k4, p1, p3tog, p1, k4, m1R, p2; rep from *.

Row 4: K2, *p5, k3, p5, k2; rep from *.

Row 5: P2, *m1L, k5, p3tog, k5, m1R, p2; rep from *.

Row 6: K2, *p6, k1, p6, k2; rep from *.

Rep Rows 1–6 for patt.

Divide for Armholes: (RS) Work 56 (64, 71, 79, 86, 94) sts as est for right front, BO 15 (14, 15, 14, 15, 14) sts, work 75 (91, 105, 121, 135, 151) sts for back, turn, leaving rem sts unworked for left front. Slip front sts to st holders or waste yarn to be worked later. Cont working on back sts only.

BACK

Note: When working armhole shaping, be sure to work corresponding increases with their decreases to maintain the correct stitch count. When only 1 inc is available per rep, work p2tog instead of p3tog. If there are not enough sts to work equal increases and decreases, work sts as they appear instead.

Shape Armholes:

Sizes 39.75 (44.75, 49.75, 54.75)" only:
Dec Row 1: (WS) K1, ssp, work as est to last 3 sts, p2tog, k1—2 sts dec'd.
Dec Row 2: (RS) P1, k2tog, work as est to last 3 sts, ssk, p1—2 sts dec'd.
Rep the last 2 rows 0 (1, 3, 5) more times—101 (113, 119, 127) sts rem.

All sizes:
Work 1 WS row as est.
Dec Row: (RS) P1, k2tog, work as est to last 3 sts, ssk, p1—2 sts dec'd.
Rep the last 2 rows 1 (4, 7, 9, 9, 9) more times—71 (81, 85, 93, 99, 107) sts rem.

Cont working as est until armholes meas 8 (8.5, 8.75, 9, 9.25, 9.75)" / 20.5 (21.5, 22, 23, 23.5, 25)cm from divide, ending after a WS row. Pm each side of center 33 (35, 35, 41, 43, 49) sts; 19 (23, 25, 26, 28, 29) sts to each side of markers.

Note: Read the following instructions before beg; shoulder and neck shaping beg at the same time.

Shape Shoulders: (RS) BO 6 (7, 8, 8, 9, 9) sts at beg of foll 4 (2, 4, 2, 4, 2) rows, then BO 7 (8, 9, 9, 10, 10) sts at beg of foll 2 (4, 2, 4, 2, 4) rows; and at the same time, on first row of shoulder shaping, work to first m, join a second ball of yarn, BO center 33 (35, 35, 41, 43, 49) sts and work to end.

RIGHT FRONT
Return held right front sts to working needle and join yarn preparing to work a WS row.

Shape Armhole:

Sizes 39.75 (44.75, 49.75, 54.75)" only:
Dec Row 1: (WS) K1, ssp, work as est to end—1 st dec'd.
Dec Row 2: (RS) Work as est to last 3 sts, ssk, p1—1 st dec'd.
Rep the last 2 rows 0 (1, 3, 5) more times—69 (75, 78, 82) sts rem.

All sizes:
Work 1 WS row as est.
Dec Row: (RS) Work as est to last 3 sts, ssk, p1—1 st dec'd.
Rep the last 2 rows 1 (4, 7, 9, 9, 9) more times—54 (59, 61, 65, 68, 72) sts rem.

Cont working as est until 3 rows are worked after the last buttonhole row, ending after a WS row.

Shape Neck: (RS) BO 13 sts, k12 then slip them to a st holder or waste yarn, BO foll 10 (11, 11, 14, 15, 18) sts and work to end—19 (23, 25, 26, 28, 29) sts rem for shoulder. Cont working in patt until armhole meas 8 (8.5, 8.75, 9, 9.25, 9.75)" / 20.5 (21.5, 22, 23, 23.5, 25)cm from dividing row, ending after a RS row.

Shape Shoulder (WS): At beg of WS rows, BO 6 (7, 8, 8, 9, 9) sts 2 (1, 2, 1, 2, 1) times, then 7 (8, 9, 9, 10, 10) sts 1 (2, 1, 2, 1, 2) times.

Sew right front shoulder sts to right back shoulder.

LEFT FRONT
Return held left front sts to working needle and join yarn preparing to work a RS row.

Next Row: (RS) BO 15 (14, 15, 14, 15, 14) sts, work to end as est—56 (64, 71, 79, 86, 94) sts rem.

Shape Armhole:

Sizes 39.75 (44.75, 49.75, 54.75)" only:
Dec Row 1: (WS) Work as est to last 3 sts, p2tog, k1—1 st dec'd.
Dec Row 2: (RS) P1, k2tog, work as est to end—1 st dec'd.
Rep the last 2 rows 0 (1, 3, 5) more times— 69 (75, 78, 82) sts rem.

All sizes:
Work 1 WS row as est.
Dec Row: (RS) P1, k2tog, work as est to end—1 st dec'd.
Rep the last 2 rows 1 (4, 7, 9, 9, 9) more times— 54 (59, 61, 65, 68, 72) sts rem.

Cont working as est until armholes meas same as right front to neck shaping, ending after a RS row.

Shape Neck (WS): BO 13 sts, k12 then slip them to a st holder or waste yarn, BO next 10 (11, 11, 14, 15, 18) sts and work to end—19 (23, 25, 26, 28, 29) sts rem for shoulder. Cont working in patt until armhole meas 8 (8.5, 8.75, 9, 9.25, 9.75)" / 20.5 (21.5, 22, 23, 23.5, 25)cm from dividing row, ending after a WS row.

Shape Shoulder (RS): At beg of RS rows, BO 6 (7, 8, 8, 9, 9) sts 2 (1, 2, 1, 2, 1) times, then 7 (8, 9, 9, 10, 10) sts 1 (2, 1, 2, 1, 2) times.

Sew left front shoulder sts to left back shoulder.

SLEEVES
With dpn and RS facing, beg at center of underarm BO, pick up and knit 7 sts along underarm BO, then 27 (29, 31, 33, 35, 37) sts to shoulder seam, pm, pick up and knit 27 (29, 31, 33, 35, 37) sts to underarm BO, pick up and knit 7 sts—68 (72, 76, 80, 84, 88) sts. Pm for beg of rnd and join to work in the rnd.

Work in 2 × 2 Rib while working as follows:

Shape Cap with Short Rows:
Short Row 1: With RS facing, work to shoulder marker, work 6 (4, 6, 4, 6, 4) sts, wrap next st and turn so WS is facing, work to shoulder marker, work 6 (4, 6, 4, 6, 4) sts, wrap next st and turn.
Short Row 2: With RS facing, *work to shoulder marker, work 10 (8, 10, 8, 10, 8) sts, wrap next st and turn; rep from * with WS facing.
Short Row 3: With RS facing, work to wrapped st, work into wrapped st, wrap next st and turn; rep from * with WS facing.
Rep Short Row 3 until only 7 sts rem unwrapped on each side of the beg of rnd marker, ending after a WS row.

Next Row: (RS) Work to end of rnd.
Cont working 2 × 2 Rib in the rnd for 3 rnds.

Shape Sleeve:

Dec Rnd: Ssk or ssp keeping in patt, work to last 2 sts, k2tog or p2tog keeping in patt—2 sts dec'd.

Rep dec rnd every 12 (10, 10, 8, 8, 8) rnds 4 (5, 5, 10, 10, 4) more times, then every 10 (8, 8, 6, 6, 6)th rnd 3 (4, 4, 1, 1, 9) times—52 (52, 56, 56, 60, 60) sts rem. Cont working even in ribbing until piece meas 16.5" / 42cm from underarm.

Dec Rnd: *K1, k2tog, k1; rep from * around—39 (39, 42, 42, 45, 45) sts rem.

Change to St st, and work 16 rnds.

Turning Rnd: *K2tog, yo; rep from * to last 1 (1, 0, 0, 1, 1) st, k1 (1, 0, 0, 1, 1). Cont in St st for 17 rnds.

Carefully fold work to the WS along turning rnd and BO while working as foll: *with LH needle, pick up a st from the WS that aligns with the next st on the LH needle, knit those 2 sts together, k1; rep from * around.

COLLAR
Return 12 held right front sts to working needle and join yarn preparing to work a RS row. Knit the held sts, then pick up and knit 10 (12, 12, 14, 16, 18) sts along right front neck BO sts, pick up and knit 1 st in corner and place a removable marker into this stitch, pick up and knit 28 sts along edge to back BO sts, 1 st in corner, pm into corner st, pick up and knit 32 (34, 34, 40, 42, 48) sts along back neck BO sts, 1 st in corner, pm into corner st, pick up and knit 28 sts along edge to front BO sts, 1 st in corner, pm into corner st, pick up and knit 10 (12, 12, 14, 16, 18) sts along left front neck BO sts, then slip 12 held left front sts to opposite end of needle, and knit across—136 (142, 142, 152, 158, 168) sts.

Purl 1 WS row.

Dec Row: (RS) *Knit to 1 st before marked corner st, remove m, sl2-k1-p2sso, replace m into the st just made; rep from * 3 more times, knit to end—128 (134, 134, 144, 150, 160) sts; 21 (23, 23, 25, 27, 29) sts each front; 26 sts along each side; 30 (32, 32, 38, 40, 46) sts along back and 4 corner sts.

Purl 1 WS row.

Turning Row: (RS) K2, yo, *[k2tog, yo] to 1 st before marked st, remove m, sl 2-k1-p2sso, replace m into the st just made, yo; rep from * 3 more times, [k2tog, yo] to last 2 sts, k2—125 (131, 131, 141, 147, 157) sts; 21 (23, 23, 27, 29) sts each front; 25 sts each side; 29 (31, 31, 37, 39, 45) sts for back and 4 corner sts.

Inc Row 1: (WS) Purl to first marked st, purl into marked st, purl to next marked st increasing 1 st between markers, purl into marked stitch; rep from * 2 more times, purl to end—128 (134, 134, 144, 150, 160) sts rem.

Inc Row 2: (RS) *Knit to marked st, remove m, inc3; replace m into yo of previous set of sts; rep from * 3 more times, knit to end—136 (142, 142, 152, 158, 168) sts.

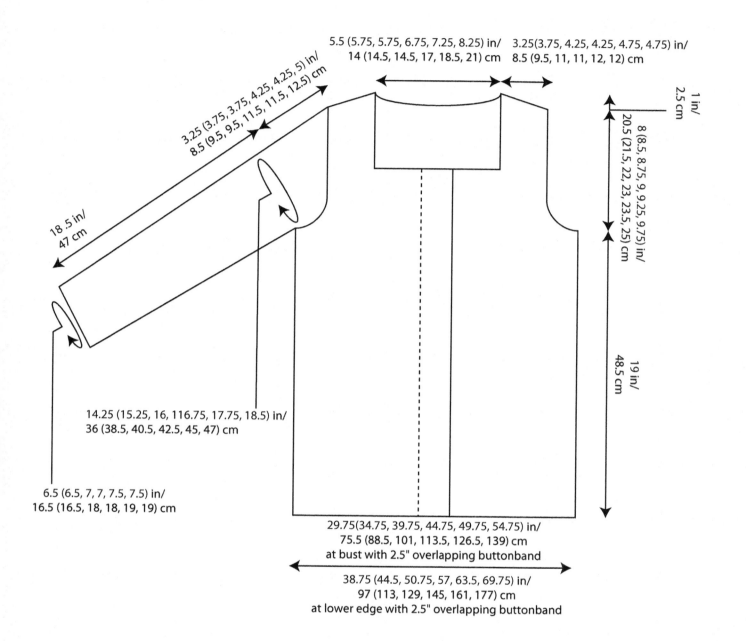

5.5 (5.75, 5.75, 6.75, 7.25, 8.25) in/
14 (14.5, 14.5, 17, 18.5, 21) cm

3.25 (3.75, 4.25, 4.25, 4.75, 4.75) in/
8.5 (9.5, 11, 11, 12, 12) cm

3.25 (3.75, 3.75, 4.25, 4.25, 5) in/
8.5 (9.5, 9.5, 11.5, 11.5, 12.5) cm

1 in/
2.5 cm

8 (8.5, 8.75, 9, 9.25, 9.75) in/
20.5 (21.5, 22, 23, 23.5, 25) cm

18 .5 in/
47 cm

19 in/
48.5 cm

14.25 (15.25, 16, 116.75, 17.75, 18.5) in/
36 (38.5, 40.5, 42.5, 45, 47) cm

6.5 (6.5, 7, 7, 7.5, 7.5) in/
16.5 (16.5, 18, 18, 19, 19) cm

29.75(34.75, 39.75, 44.75, 49.75, 54.75) in/
75.5 (88.5, 101, 113.5, 126.5, 139) cm
at bust with 2.5" overlapping buttonband

38.75 (44.5, 50.75, 57, 63.5, 69.75) in/
97 (113, 129, 145, 161, 177) cm
at lower edge with 2.5" overlapping buttonband

Purl 1 WS row.

Joining Row: Fold work to the WS along turning row, BO all sts while working as foll: *with LH needle, pick up a st from WS of body that aligns with the next st on the LH needle, knit those 2 sts together, k1; rep from * around.

FINISHING

Fold front facing to WS, folding along the turning st, and sew in place using mattress stitch.

Lower Right Front Trim: With crochet hook and RS facing, join yarn to lower right front edge through both layers of fabric, and sc evenly along hem to the CO sts. Fasten off. Weave in end so the crochet trim appears to flow into the slipped turning stitch.

Upper Right Front Trim: With crochet hook and RS facing, join yarn to collar at pick up row, sc evenly along collar to turning row. Fasten off. Weave in the tail at the beg of the collar in a way that appears as though the slipped turning stitch and the crochet trim flow together.

Lower Left Front Trim: With WS facing, work as for lower right front trim.

Upper Left Front Trim: With WS facing, work as for upper right front trim.

Reinforce buttonholes by working whip stitch through both layers of fabric around the buttonhole. Sew buttons opposite buttonholes.

Weave in ends. Block to measurements.

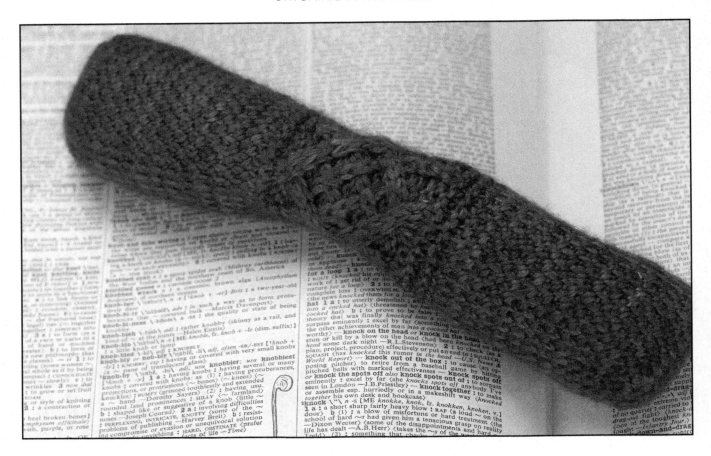

L.O.C. BOOKWEIGHT
BY KENDRA NITTA

Bookmarks help you remember your page when your book is closed; bookweights keep your book open at that page. They're especially useful for gently holding open paperback books without having to break the spine—perfect if you're trying to read while your hands are full of knitting needles and yarn.

The twisted stitches of Kendra Nitta's bookweight were inspired by a painted border running across the archways at the Library of Congress. It's worked in the round from the outer edges, then filled with rice or small pebbles before the center is finished. Because it's small and because gauge can be a bit flexible, it's ideal for using up leftover yarn from larger projects.

SIZE
One size

FINISHED MEASUREMENTS
(before stuffing)
Width: 2.5" / 6.5cm
Length: 9" / 23cm

MATERIALS
Artfibers Carezza [30% silk, 30% baby alpaca, 40% extrafine merino; 265 yds / 242m per 50g skein]; color #12 (rust); 1 skein

2 16-inch US #3 / 3.25mm circular needles
2 16-inch US #4 / 3.5mm circular needles

Cable needle
Darning needle
Beans or other small heavy weights

GAUGE

32 sts and 40 rows = 4" / 10cm in St st
44 sts and 68 rows = 4" / 10cm in Plaited Basket Stitch
on smaller needles

PATTERN

Using Judy's Magic Cast On (see knitty.com/
ISSUEspring06/FEATmagiccaston.html), CO 22 sts onto
each of two smaller circular needles—44 sts.

Rnd 1: *M1, RT to end of needle, m1; rep from * on
second needle—48 sts.
Rnd 2: *M1, LT to end of needle, m1; rep from * on
second needle—52 sts.
Rep Rnds 1 & 2 once more—60 sts.

Work in Plaited Basket Stitch:
Rnd 1: RT to end.
Rnd 2: Ktbl, LT until 1 st rem, ktbl.
Rep Rnds 1 & 2 until piece measures 3.5" / 9cm from
CO, ending with Rnd 2.

Next rnd: Join a second strand and k2tog to end, holding
yarn doubled—30 sts.
Purl 1 rnd.

If you will be seaming with kitchener stitch, place sts on
holder; otherwise, BO purlwise.

Rep for second end, but do not place sts on holder or
BO after purl rnd. Knit 1 rnd, purl 1 rnd.

CENTER

Change to larger needles and work Rnds 1–15 of chart,
continuing to work double-stranded.

Purl 1 rnd; knit 1 rnd.

If you will be seaming with kitchener stitch, place sts on
holder; otherwise, BO.

FINISHING

Weave in ends and steam block both pieces. Using
double strand of yarn, seam about three-quarters of the
way around piece with kitchener stitch or mattress stitch.
Stop and fill, using a funnel if desired. Lay flat to keep
filling in while seaming rem sts.

Chart columns numbered 15 14 13 12 11 10 9 8 7 6 5 4 3 2 1; rows numbered 1–15.

Chart Legend

Symbol	Name	Instructions
•	**purl**	purl stitch
᠔	**k1 elongated**	knit one stitch wrapping yarn twice. Drop extra wrap from needle on next row.
⅄⅄	**Right Twist**	Skip the first stitch, knit into 2nd stitch, then knit skipped stitch. Slip both stitches from needle together OR k2tog leaving sts on LH needle, then k first st again, sl both sts off needle.
⟋⟍	**c2 over 2 left**	sl 2 to CN, hold in front. k2, k2 from CN
⟍⟋	**c2 over 1 right P**	sl1 to CN, hold in back. k2, p1 from CN
⟋⟍	**c2 over 1 left P**	sl2 to CN, hold in front. p1, k2 from CN
⅄⅄	**c2 over 1 right**	sl1 to CN, hold in back. k2, k1 from CN
⟋⟍	**c2 over 1 left**	sl2 to CN, hold in front. k1, k2 from CN
⟍⟋	**Left Twist, purl bg**	sl1 to CN, hold in front. p1. k1 from CN
⟋⟍	**Right Twist, purl bg**	sl1 to CN, hold in back. k1, p1 from CN
⟍⟋	**Left Twist**	sl1 to CN, hold in front. k1, k1 from CN

STUDY SESSION
BY CAROL FELLER

Beloved second home to scholars of all ages, the library has virtually everything a researcher needs—but you will need to bring your own pens and pencils. Take them along for the ride in Carol Feller's rustic pencil case. Small enough to fit in your backpack but large enough to accommodate virtually all your homework accessories, Study Session will prove surprisingly useful. A simple slip-stitch pattern combined with a tweedy yarn create a durable but attractive case, and the button closure means you won't have to fuss with a zipper.

SIZE
One size

FINISHED MEASUREMENTS
Length: 7.75" / 19.5cm
Circumference: 10" / 25.5cm

MATERIALS
Cushendale Woollen Mills 4-ply/Sport [100% wool;
367 yds / 339m per 113g skein]
• [MC] Silver; 1 skein
• [CC] Autumn; 1 skein
Only 10g of contrasting color was used.

1 set US #2 / 2.75mm double-point needles
1 set US #2 / 2.75mm straight needles

Yarn needle
Stitch marker
3 shanked buttons, approx ½" / 1 cm in diameter

GAUGE
25 sts and 32 rows = 4" / 10cm in St st
26 sts and 48 rows = 4" / 10cm in patt stitch

PATTERN NOTES
Pearl Tweed:
Row 1 (RS): With CC, k2, [sl2 wyif, k1] to last st, k2.
Row 2 (WS): With CC, p2, [k1, p1, sl1 wyif] to last st, p2.
Row 3: With MC, k4, [sl1 wyib, k2] to last 3 sts, sl1, k2.
Row 4: With MC, purl.
Row 5: With CC, k3, [sl2 wyif, k1] to last st, k1.
Row 6: With CC, p3, [sl1 wyif, k1, p1] to last st, p1.
Row 7: With MC, k2, [sl1 wyib, k2] to last st, k2.
Row 8: With MC, purl.
Row 9: With CC, k2, sl1 wyif, [k1, sl2 wyif] to last 4 sts, k1, sl 1, k2.
Row 10: With CC, p2, [sl1 wyif, k1, p1] to last 2 sts, p2.
Row 11: With MC, k3, [sl1 wyib, k2] to last st, k1.
Row 12: With MC, purl.
Rep Rows 1–12 for patt.

I-Cord Bind Off:
CO 3 sts at start of row, [k2, ssk, place all 3 sts back on LH needle] until all sts have been worked. Three i-cord sts rem on needle when finished. K3tog, break yarn and draw through final st.

I-Cord Buttonhole:
[On 2 dpns, knit 3 sts, slip 3 sts just worked from right to LH needle and tug yarn snugly] until i-cord is desired length. Button length worked in sample is approx ½" / 1 cm.

PATTERN
BODY
With MC, CO 52 sts. Work in garter stitch (knit every row) until piece measures approx 1" / 2.5cm.

Work in Pearl Tweed for 3 patt reps (36 rows); work will measure approx 4" / 10cm. Using MC, work in St st for 3" / 7.5cm.

Work in Pearl Tweed for 3 patt repeats (36 rows); work will measure approx 9" / 23cm in total. Using MC, work in St st for 1" / 2.5cm.

BO 11 sts using i-cord bind off, [work i-cord buttonhole, BO 15 sts using i-cord bind off] twice, work i-cord buttonhole, BO rem 11 sts using i-cord bind off.

SIDES
Fold first and last inch over each other and pin in position with buttonholes on outside.

Using dpn, pick up 60 sts evenly around the edge of the piece, picking up sts from both top and bottom layer at the same time where they fold over each other.

Knit 1 rnd.

Dec Rnd 1: [K8, k2tog, pm] around—6 sts dec'd.
Dec Rnd 2: [Knit to last 2 sts before m, k2tog] around—6 sts dec'd.
Cont to work Dec Rnd 2 until 6 sts rem; remove m.

Final Rnd: [K2tog] 3 times—3 sts.

Break yarn, draw through remaining sts using tapestry needle and fasten securely.

Rep for second end of pencil case.

FINISHING
Weave in all loose ends.

Sew buttons into position. Block piece to dimensions given, it may help to stuff the pencil case so that it hold its shape while drying.

SECTION 5: STAFF ROOM

COFFEE PRESS COZY

BY SUSAN DITTRICH

What happens in the back offices of a library? Well, plenty of coffee drinking. And because librarians often get called away to deal with patrons and other library issues, the coffee could get cold—and no one wants to deal with a librarian who hasn't had enough coffee.

Susan Dittrich has fashioned a helpful compromise between service and addiction. Her French press coffee cozy sports the Dewey call number for coffee on one side and the Library of Congress classification on the other, thus making it appropriate for librarians who work in a variety of settings. Other professions won't be left out in the cold, though—this cozy works for coffee mavens of all stripes.

SIZE
One size

FINISHED MEASUREMENTS
The coffee press cozy measures 11.75" × 5.75" / 30cm × 14.5cm when tube is flattened. The cozy will fit a coffee press with a 12" / 30.5cm circumference (such as a Bodum 8-cup [34 oz / 1l] model).

MATERIALS
Brown Sheep Nature Spun Sport [100% wool; 184 yds / 168m per 50g skein]
- [MC] Butterfly Blue; 1 skein
- [CC1] Spiced Plum; 1 skein
- [CC2] Bamboo; 1 skein
- [CC3] Aran; 1 skein

1 set US #1 / 2.25mm double-point needles, or size needed to obtain gauge (or use one long circular for magic loop or two circulars, as you prefer)

Yarn needle

GAUGE
32 sts and 40 rows = 4" / 10cm in St st

PATTERN
With MC, CO 90 sts and distribute evenly on the needles. Join for working in the round, being careful not to twist. Note or mark beg of the rnd.

Rnd 1: Purl.
Rnd 2: Knit.
Rnd 3: Purl.
Rnds 4–7: Knit.

Work charts as follows:
Rnds 1–7: Work Chart 1 to m; work Chart 2 to end.
Rnds 8–10: With MC, knit 3 rnds.
Rnds 11–17: Work Chart 2 to m; work Chart 3 to end.
Rnds 18–22: Knit with MC.

Work these 22 rnds 4 more times.

With MC, purl 1 rnd, knit 1 rnd, purl 1 rnd.

BO all sts.

I-cord ties (make 6):
Using CC1 and dpns, CO 3 sts. *Do not turn work. Slide 3 sts to other end of needle and k3 sts. Rep from * until i-cord measures approx 6" / 15cm long or desired length. Cut yarn. Using a yarn needle, draw tail through 3 live sts, then thread both tails down into the center of the i-cord.

FINISHING
Flatten the tube, making sure the writing is centered on both sides, and block the coffee cozy to finished measurements.

When dry, pin 3 i-cords to each open end along the inside edge of the tube; 1 in the center, 1 at the top and 1 at the bottom.

Using a tapestry needle and MC, stitch the open ends shut, removing the pins holding the i-cord ties as you come to them.

Reinforce the stitching in the area where the i-cords are attached.

CHART 1

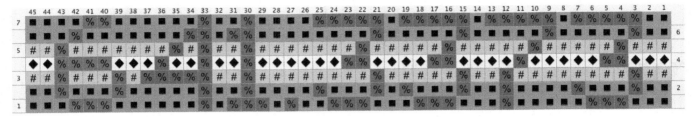

CHART 2

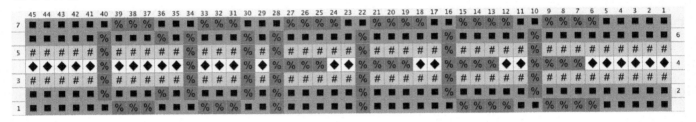

CHART 3

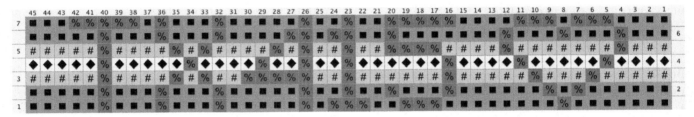

■ MC

% CC1

CC2

◆ CC3

STEREOTYPICAL
BY HOLLY CHAYES

Plenty of librarians have 20/20 vision. But then again, plenty don't. If you're one who needs a soft, safe place for her specs, Holly Chayes' colorwork case may be just the thing. Stereotypical is cleverly constructed in one piece, with the Fair Isle exterior and a laceweight lining worked as two sections of a closed tube which folds in on itself. Vivid colors breathe new life into the classic argyle pattern and make this case a nerd chic statement. Your glasses may be stereotypical, but their case doesn't have to be.

SIZE
One size

FINISHED MEASUREMENTS
Width: 4" / 10cm
Height after folding: 8" / 20.5cm
Height before folding: 15.75" / 40cm

MATERIALS
[MC] Cascade Heritage [75% superwash merino, 25% nylon; 437 yds / 400m per 100g skein]; color: #5629 light green; 1 skein
[CC1] Cascade Heritage [75% superwash merino, 25% nylon; 437 yds / 400m per 100g skein]; color: #5650 purple; 1 skein

[CC2] Cascade Alpaca Lace [100% Baby Alpaca; 437 yds / 400m per 50g skein]; color: #1421 Spring Green; 1 skein

1 set US #2.5 / 3mm double-point needles (magic loop or 2-circulars techniques can be used)

Yarn needle

GAUGE

40 sts and 40 rows = 4" / 10cm in washed and blocked patt stitch
26 sts and 40 rows = 4" / 10cm in St st in single color, after washing and blocking

PATTERN NOTES

Chart repeat is worked twice per round.
Weaving in ends as you go makes finishing much easier.

PATTERN

Using Judy's Magic Cast On (see knitty.com/ISSUEspring06/FEATmagiccaston.html) and MC, CO 74 sts over 2 dpns.

Attach CC1. Work Chart Rnds 1–4 once.
Work Chart Rnds 5–22 three times (as shown by red box).
Work Chart Rnds 23–39 once. Break CC1.
With MC, purl 1 rnd, then knit 1 rnd. Break MC.
Holding CC2 double, knit 2 rnds.
Next Rnd (still in CC2): [Ssk, k5, s2kp, k7, sk2p, k7, sk2p, k5, k2tog] twice—58 sts.
Work even in St st for 7" / 18cm.

FINISHING

Weave in all ends, if not previously woven in.
Graft end closed.
Weave in final end. Block lightly.
Fold laceweight half into fair isle half along purl ridge.

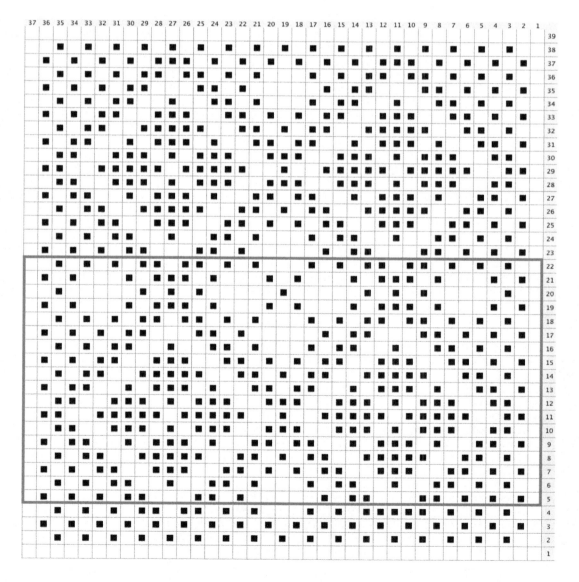

simply can't ... too abomi-
nable." As ... answer to
the bell: " ... entlemen,
when you ... coats for
Mr. Robe... rts had
locked u...

Bella: " ... Mr. Camp-
bell said ... didn't be-
lieve Mrs ... e like it,
ma'am, ... hesitates,
and Mrs ... her feet,
with arm...

Mrs. ... ma'am, I
Bella: ... things fly
couldn'...
about a...
Mrs. R...
Mrs. C... e gentlemen
Bella: " ... that them-
would have...

"THAT LITTLE SUPPER"

BIBLIORT
BY SHARON FULLER

The library world is full of urban legends about things found in returned books that were presumably used as bookmarks. Known in the trade as "bibliorts," they range from the charming to the bizarre: leaves, money, old postcards, small bags of drugs, slices of cheese and bacon, and other bits of ephemera from readers' lives.

Here, Sharon Fuller imagines the bibliort as a lacy garter belt (you can imagine for yourself who left it and in what kind of book). Not only is it pretty but it serves it purpose well, the delicate ribbon keeping your page for you while the lacy panel reminds you that this is a book you want to get back to.

SIZE
As desired—see below.

FINISHED MEASUREMENTS
Knit to desired dimensions. Sample measurements are:
- Bibelot (to fit ankle): 1.25 × 3.75" / 3 × 9.5cm (with ribbon, garter circumference is 10" / 25.5cm unstretched or 11" / 28cm stretched)
- Pulp (to fit lower thigh): 1.5 × 5" / 4 × 12.5cm (with ribbon, garter circumference is 12.5" / 32cm unstretched or 15" / 38cm stretched)
- Trade (to fit upper thigh): 1.5 × 6.75" / 4 × 17cm (with elastic, garter circumference is 17" / 43cm unstretched or 21" / 53.5cm stretched)

MATERIALS
Just about any springy, fingering-weight yarn will work for this pattern. You can use either plain or elasticized ribbon, depending on how much stretch you want. All versions of the pattern use only a small portion of the skein.

Bibelot:
- [MC] Kollage Sock-a-Licious [70% superwash wool, 10% mulberry silk, 20% nylon; 350 yds / 318m per 100g skein]; color: #7820 Marshmallow; 1 skein
- [CC] Alpha Fashion Fiber Doublefaced Silk Satin ¼-inch (6mm) ribbon; color: Wine (17)

Pulp:
- [MC] Yarn Love Joan of Arc [50% merino, 50% Tencel; 410 yds / 373m per 113g skein]; color: Champagne; 1 skein
- [CC] May Arts Faux Suede Ruffle Edge ⅝-inch (15mm) ribbon; color: NV33 (brown)

Pulp (white):
- [MC] Kollage Sock-a-Licious [70% superwash wool, 10% mulberry silk, 20% nylon; 350 yds / 318m per 100g skein]; color: #7820 Marshmallow; 1 skein
- [CC] Stephanie de Rubans 25mm ruffled elastic ribbon; color: ivory

Trade:
- M&K Alpaca Silk [70% baby alpaca, 30% silk; 220 yds / 200m per 50g ball]; color: #711 silver; 1 skein
- Stephanie de Rubans 25mm ruffled elastic ribbon; color: ivory

Pattern is written for the magic loop technique on one long circular needle, but can easily be adapted for dpns or two circulars.

US #1 / 2.25mm circular needle
US #1½ / 2.5mm circular needle
US #4 / 3.5mm needle, any type (for binding off)

Yarn needle
Sewing needle and coordinating thread
2 small buttons needed for Pulp (white) version

GAUGE
Gauge is not critical. Bookmark length is determined by your gauge and the number of picots you cast on. Fit can be adjusted by changing the ribbon length.

PATTERN NOTES
Bookmark is worked in the round from the outside in, and bound off down the middle.

Where more than one number is listed, first number is for Bibelot, and numbers in brackets are for Pulp and Trade. Where only one number is listed, it applies to all sizes.

Cable Cast On:

Make a slip knot and place loop over needle. Insert RH needle through first st from front to back and knit 1. *Insert RH needle from front to back between the last 2 sts on the LH needle. Knit 1. Rep from * until desired number of sts have been cast on.

Picot Cast On:

CO 4 sts using cable cast on. Knit into the last st cast on. Knit into the next st on the LH needle and pass previous stitch over. 1 st bound off—3 sts rem from the picot. Rep until desired number of sts have been cast on.

S2kp: Slip 2 as if to knit together, knit next st, pass two slipped sts over. If you are working at a tight gauge for your yarn, you may find it easier to slip the right-most st over first, and then the other st.

Twisted Rib: [K1tbl, p1] around.

One-Row Buttonhole:

1. (RS) Bring yarn to front, sl 1, take yarn to back. [Sl 1 and pass previous slipped st over] until desired number of sts have been bound off. Sl last bound-off st back to LH needle. Turn work.
2. (WS) Snug yarn and, using cable cast-on, CO one more stitch than you bound off. Turn work, leaving yarn hanging to WS.
3. (RS) Sl extra cast-on st and last bound off st onto RH needle. Slip cast-on st over to close the buttonhole.

Three-Needle Bind Off:

*Bring work to tips of both needles and hold needles parallel next to each other. Put a third needle through the front of the first st on the front needle and the back of the st (from your point of view) on the back needle. Knit these two sts together. Rep from *, slipping prior st over the st just worked—1 st bound off. Continue in this manner until all sts have been bound off.

PATTERN

Using picot cast on, and US #1½ needle, CO 72 (126, 174) sts—that is, 24 (42, 58) picots. Divide sts evenly and join to work in the round, being careful not to twist.

Rnd 1: Knit.

Rnd 2: Switch to smallest needle. [S2kp, yo], rep to end of rnd—48 (84, 116) or two-thirds of original sts rem.

Rnd 3: Knit.

Bibelot size:

Rnd 4: Work 1 rnd in twisted rib.

Rnd 5: K1tbl, p1, skp, k1tbl, p1, k1tbl, k2tog; cont in patt to end of needle. Rep for second needle—4 sts dec'd.

Rnd 6: K1tbl, p1, skp, p1, k2tog; cont in patt to end of needle. Rep for second needle—4 sts dec'd.

Larger sizes:

Buttonholes are optional for larger sizes, depending on how you want to thread the ribbon. Work buttonhole over 6 or 8 sts, based on the width of your buttons or ribbon. To work single buttonholes, rather than sets of two, work Rnd 4 in twisted rib, and work the buttonholes on Rnd 5 only. To omit all buttonholes, work both rounds in twisted rib.

Rnds 7–8 (4–5, 4–5): K1tbl, p1; work one-row buttonhole; cont in twisted rib to end of needle. Rep for second needle.

Rnd 9 (6, 6): K1tbl, p1, knit to 2 sts before center of buttonhole, k2tog, pm, skp, knit to end of buttonhole; cont in twisted rib to end of needle. Rep for second needle—4 sts dec'd.

Rnds 10–11 (7–8, 7–8): K1tbl, p1, knit to 2 sts before m, k2tog, sl m, skp, knit to end of buttonhole; cont in twisted rib to end of needle. Rep for second needle— 4 sts dec'd per round.

Bind off: Work in twisted rib to first m. Move beg of round to the left and set middle of rnd at second m. Using largest needle, work three-needle bind off. Thread yarn through last st and pull to WS.

FINISHING

Weave in ends and block. Thread ribbon as shown, or as desired. If using wider ribbon and buttonholes, turn under raw edges and sew ribbon to secure. Sew buttons to end of ribbon if desired.

EX LIBRIS
BY SHARON FULLER

In ancient times, cuneiform tablets were kept safe in earthenware jars and papyrus scrolls were housed in leather or clay tubes. Today, the amount of information in a single slim e-reader can rival that of any Mesopotamian library, but it still needs protecting.

Sharon Fuller took the traditional book plate and worked it into a pretty, practical e-reader cozy. Worked entirely in stockinette stitch with duplicate stitch letters, it's also a quick and easy project. Since the optional monogram makes it customizable, it makes a lovely, personalized present for the e-book addict in your life.

SIZES
Multiple sizes for Kindle and Nook e-readers. (Sample worked in Size 1.)

FINISHED MEASUREMENTS
Size 1: 4.5 × 6.5" / 11.5 × 16.5cm (e.g. Kindle)
Size 2: 4.75 × 6.75" / 12 × 17cm (e.g. Kindle Touch)
Size 3: 4.75 × 7.5" / 12 × 19cm (e.g. Kindle Fire or Keyboard)
Size 4: 5 × 6.5" / 12.5 × 16.5cm (e.g. Nook Simple Touch)
Size 5: 5 × 8" / 12.5 × 20.5cm (e.g. Nook Color)

MATERIALS
Cascade Heritage Sock [100% superwash merino wool; 437 yds / 400m per 100g skein]
• [MC] #5663 Wine; 1 skein
• [CC] #5645 Tangerine; 1 skein
Approx 115–200 yds / 105–183m of MC are needed, depending on size, and up to 45 yds / 41m of CC.

Pattern is written for the magic loop technique on one long circular needle, but can easily be adapted for double-point needles or two circulars. Double-point needles are needed only to work applied i-cord.

US #1 / 2.25mm circular needle
1 set US #1 / 2.25mm double-point needles
1 set US #1½ / 2.5mm double-point needles

Waste yarn
Yarn needle
Button, sewing needle, thread, and scrap of felt or fleece

GAUGE
32 sts and 46 rnds = 4" / 10cm in St st
The same gauge is assumed for the body knit in the round as for the flap worked back and forth. If your gauge differs significantly between the two methods, you may need to adjust needle size for the flap.

PATTERN NOTES
If you do not own a gadget of the type for which you are knitting a cover, mock one up by cutting 2–3 pieces of corrugated cardboard to the stated dimensions, wrapping the pieces together in a sheet of paper and taping the paper in place. Periodically use this insert to make sure that your work is an appropriate size.

I-cord is worked on larger needles across the live sts so the row gauge of the i-cord will be closer to the stitch gauge of the edge, and not pull it too tight. Return to smaller needles for edging the flap because you will be working one row of i-cord per flap row.

Backward Loop Cast On: Loop working yarn and place it on needle backward so that it doesn't unwind. Rep until desired number of sts have been cast on.

Ssp (slip, slip, purl): Sl 1 st knitwise, sl next st knitwise. Return slipped sts to LH needle. Insert RH needle left to right from behind into back loops of the 2 sts and purl them tog—1 st dec'd.

PATTERN
Where more than one number is listed, first number is for Size 1; the numbers in brackets are for the larger sizes. Where only one number is listed, it applies to all sizes.

BODY
Rnd 1: Using Judy's Magic Cast On (see knitty.com/ISSUEspring06/FEATmagiccaston.html), CO 78 (82, 82, 86, 86) sts. There will be 39 (41, 41, 43, 43) on each needle. Cast-on edge will count as the first rnd.

Rnd 2: Knit around, working into wrong side of cast-on sts, so purl bump of cast on faces to RS of work.

Rnd 3: Knit to end of first needle, CO 1 st using backward loop cast on. Rep on second needle—2 sts inc'd.

Rnd 4: Knit to 1 st before end of first needle, p1. Rep on second needle.
Rep Rnd 4 until a total of 78 (82, 90, 78, 97) rnds have been worked.

Slip last st from previous rnd back on to first needle. Knit to 1 st before end of first needle, p1—41 (43, 43, 45, 45) sts on needle. Place sts from second needle onto waste yarn.

FLAP
Work flap back and forth on rem sts.
Row 1 (WS): P1, p2tog, purl to last 3 sts, ssp, p1—39 (41, 41, 43, 43) sts.
Row 2 (RS): Knit.
Row 3: As for Row 1—37 (39, 39, 41, 41) sts.
Row 4: Knit.
Row 5: Purl.
Row 6: Knit.
Row 7: P1, p2tog, purl to last 3 sts, ssp, p1—2 sts dec'd.

Rep Rows 4–7 until 5 (5, 5, 7, 3) sts rem.
Work Rows 4–6 one more time.
BO rem sts in purl, working last st into row below.

EDGING: APPLIED I-CORD
Return edge sts from waste yarn to needle.

Using Judy's Magic Cast On, CO 6 sts in CC onto two larger dpns. Put the 3 sts from bottom needle on waste yarn. Slide work to other end of needle.

Rnd 1: Bring yarn behind work and knit across. With WS of cover facing, knit into first live st. Slide.
Rnd 2: Bring yarn behind work. K3, sl last st knitwise. Knit into next live st, psso. Slide.
Rep Rnd 2 until all live sts have been worked. (When working live sts, you may find it easier to slip the i-cord sts onto the needle carrying the edge sts after each rnd.)

Switch to smaller dpns and cont in this manner around the flap, picking up 1 st per row.

When you reach the tip of the flap, work i-cord without picking up sts until your have an appropriate length of button loop for your button.

Cont applied i-cord up other side of flap.
After last rnd of i-cord, graft live sts together with cast-on sts from waste yarn.

DUPLICATE STITCH PATTERN
Duplicate stitch is a method of applying contrast color by using a yarn needle and contrasting color to trace the path of existing knit stitches.

You may find it easier to count sts if you weave thread through the fabric to mark 10-stitch squares, as marked on the chart. The first chart row corresponds to the cast-on sts.

Cut working yarn to about an arm's length. Don't succumb to the temptation to cut it longer so as to have fewer ends to weave in. Longer yarn takes longer to sew, is more apt to tangle, and puts more wear on both the fabric and the sewing yarn.

Let the yarn and needle dangle from the work periodically to untwist.

Work duplicate stitch at the same gauge as the knit fabric. For chart sts marked with a V, trace the entire st. For sts marked with a \ or /, trace only the left (/) or right (\) leg of the st.
Work in rows, rather than columns, where possible. The uprights of the capital letters, for example, will lie flatter if you work in rows instead of three separate columns.

To get the columns of half-stitches on either edge to match, you may need to apply extra twist to the yarn for the left-leaning sts and untwist the yarn for the right-leaning sts.

Keep yarn ends out of your way while you work by bringing each new strand of yarn in from the RS at the edge of the work, and finishing the tail end by bringing it back to the outside.

If you need to undo sts, it is generally easier to do so from the tail end of the yarn, rather than the beginning. Sometimes sewn sts get split by later sts, which makes them impossible to unpick by working from the beg.

Wait until you are completely done to weave in ends, in case you later find you need to change a stitch or two.

FINISHING
Weave in ends and block.

Attach button: Use sewing needle and thread to sew a small piece of felt or fleece to WS of back of work at location where button will be attached. Attach button, sewing through work and backing fabric. If button does not have a shank, create a thread shank of an appropriate length.

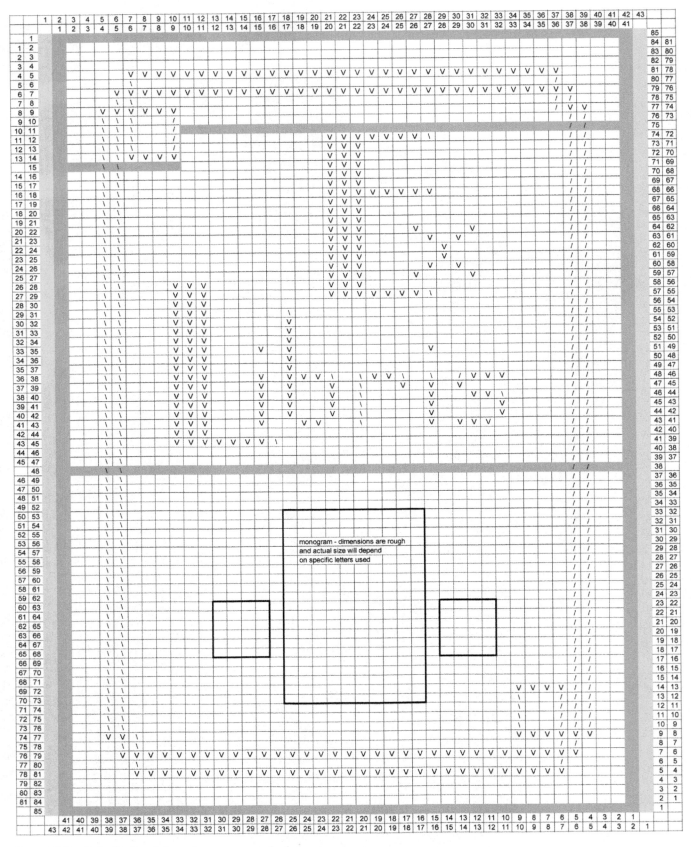

monogram - dimensions are rough
and actual size will depend
on specific letters used

Size 1 (Kindle): Omit pink and orange rows/columns.

Size 2 (Kindle Touch): Omit orange columns.

Size 4 (Nook Simple Touch): Omit pink rows/columns.

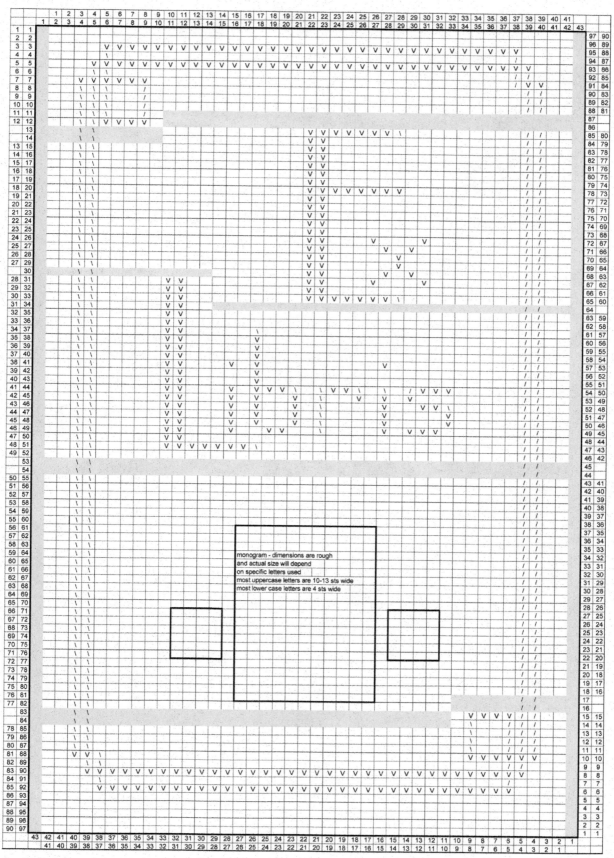

Size 3 (Kindle KB and Fire): Omit green rows/columns.
Size 5 (Nook Color): Work all rows/columns.

ATHENA'S BOOKENDS
BY KENDRA NITTA

O wls have been a symbol of learning since ancient times when they were associated with Athena, goddess of wisdom. The cunning little owls on Kendra Nitta's bookends have wise advice, indeed: *Read.*

And while you're at it, add some whimsy to your library with this set of Arts and Crafts-inspired Fair Isle bookend cozies. Worked in the round with little finishing required, they're a great project for stranded knitting novices and experts alike, and would make a delightful gift for your favorite bibliophile.

SIZE
One size

FINISHED MEASUREMENTS
Width: 5.25" / 13.5cm
Length: 5.5" / 14cm

MATERIALS
Spud and Chloe Fine [80% superwash wool, 20% silk; 248 yds / 227m per 65g skein]
- [MC] #7803 Dachshund; 1 skein
- [CC1] #7804 Cricket; 1 skein
- [CC2] #7801 Glow Worm; 1 skein
- [CC3] #7801 Clementine; 1 skein
- [CC4] #7800 Popcorn; 1 skein

Approx yardage requirements: MC: 115 yds / 105m; CC1: 40 yds / 37m; CC2: 40 yds / 37m; CC2: 10 yds / 9m; CC3: 20 yds / 18m.

US #2½ / 3mm circular needles—either long circular, 2 short circulars, or double-point needles, as you prefer
1 set US #1½ / 2.5mm double-point needles

Yarn needle
Two 5" / 12.5cm metal bookends

GAUGE
32 sts and 34 rows = 4" / 10cm in stranded St st
Because gauge may differ between colorways of the same yarn, swatch using multiple colors to best determine needle size.

PATTERN NOTES
When working duplicate stitch detailing, use a long length of yarn and work side to side, periodically weave into the wrong side rather than breaking the yarn after each individual stitch.

PATTERN
Using MC, larger needles, and a provisional cast on, CO 82 sts. Join to work in the round, being careful not to twist.

Work Rnds 1–42 of chart, but do not break yarn. Carefully turn piece inside out. Using MC and dpn, seam using 3-needle bind off. Work second bookend as first.

FINISHING
Using CC3 and tapestry needle, work duplicate st as indicated, starting from the top right corner of the chart (see Pattern Notes). Rep with MC for rem sts.

Carefully remove waste yarn from provisional CO and place resulting 82 sts onto one circular needle. Using MC and smaller-size dpns, CO 3 sts. Do not turn, but slide all 3 sts on dpn to beg of dpn.

With owl side facing so that the owl motif appears upside-down, start at right edge and work applied i-cord as foll: *K2 from dpn, sl last st purlwise, k1 from circular needle, psso. Do not turn work, but slide all 3 sts on dpn back to beg of dpn. Rep from *, working all sts from circular needle.

When all sts are worked, work one more row of i-cord, then BO.

FINISHING
Seam sides neatly together. Work second bookend as first.

Weave in ends. Block flat or over metal bookends covered with foil to prevent rusting.

■ MC
% CC₁
CC₂
CC₃
☐ CC₄

☐ work in color shown in center of box;
duplicate stitch afterward with CC₃

work in color shown in center of box;
duplicate stitch afterward with MC

— divide between front and back of
bookend cover

GRANDE
DIZIONARIO
DELLA LINGUA
ITALIANA

GRAN
DIZIONA
DELLA LIN
ITALIA

BOOKWORM
BY CHEEZOMBIE, AKA KAHRA GRAEBNER

Much cuter—and more literate—than your average bug, Cheezombie's adorable little bookworm is equally at home tucked away on a high shelf reading bodice rippers or hanging out on the Children's Reference Desk sharing *Goodnight Moon* with the preschoolers.

Bookworm is knit in the round with bits of worsted-weight yarn and is ideal for using up scraps. He's a simple knit, his shaping accomplished with strategically placed increases and decreases, plus a few short rows in the "chest" area. He can be easily made huge and huggable or tiny and adorable by substituting different yarn weights and needle sizes. Regardless of size, he will delight readers young and old.

SIZE
One size

FINISHED MEASUREMENTS
7" / 18cm long × 3" / 7.5cm tall

MATERIALS
Approx. 38 yds / 35m worsted-weight (8- or 10-ply) yarn in worm color; and scraps of white, black, and book cover color yarn

Yarn used in model:
- Eyeballs/book pages: KnitPicks Bare Worsted [100% superwash merino wool; 220 yds / 200m per 100g skein]; color: Bare; 1 skein
- Body/arms: Stitch Nation by Debbie Stoller Bamboo Ewe [55% bamboo viscose, 45% wool; 177 yds / 162m per 100g ball]; color: Sprout; 1 ball
- Book cover: KnitPicks Wool of the Andes [100% Peruvian Highland wool; 110 yds / 100m per 50g ball]; color: Cranberry; 1 ball

1 set US #3 / 3.25mm double-point needles, or size needed to obtain gauge

Plastic pellets, beads, or other weighted material
Poly-fil or other stuffing
Yarn needle

GAUGE
Exact gauge is unnecessary, but it should be tight enough that stuffing does not poke through. Using needles a few sizes smaller than recommended for the yarn will give a tighter fabric.

PATTERN NOTES
LLI: Left Lifted Increase: using the LH needle, pick up loop from stitch 2 rows below the last stitch on the RH needle and knit through the back loop.

RLI: Right Lifted Increase: using RH needle, pick up loop from stitch 1 row below the next stitch on the LH needle and knit.

PATTERN
BODY
The body is worked from the tail to the head. With worm color yarn, CO 6 sts, distribute on needles and join into round.

Rnd 1: Knit.
Rnd 2: [K1, LLI] to end—12 sts.
Rnd 3: Knit.
Rnd 4: [RLI, k6, LLI] to end—16 sts.

Rnd 5: Knit.
Rnd 6: [RLI, k8, LLI] to end—20 sts.
Rnds 7–16: Knit.

Rnd 17: RLI, k8, k2tog, ssk, k8, LLI.
Rnd 18: Knit.
Rnd 19: As for Rnd 17.
Rnd 20: Knit.

Rnd 21: As for Rnd 17.
Rnds 22–27: Knit.
Rnd 28: Ssk, k8, LLI, RLI, k8, k2tog.

Rnd 29: Knit.
Rnd 30: As for Rnd 28.
Rnd 31: Knit.
Rnd 32: As for Rnd 28.
Rnds 33–40: Knit.

Close the small opening at the cast-on end of the tail & fill the end with plastic pellets or other weighted material. Stuff the rest of the body with polyfil or other soft material. Continue stuffing as you go.

Rnds 41–45: K15, w&t, p10, w&t, k15.
Rnds 46–59: Knit.
Rnd 60: K3, k2tog, ssk, k6, k2tog, ssk, k3—16 sts.
Rnd 61: K2, k2tog, ssk, k4, k2tog, ssk, k2—12 sts.
Rnd 62: K1, k2tog, ssk, k2, k2tog, ssk, k1—8 sts.

Cut yarn, draw through rem sts, and pull tight. Weave in end.

EYEBALLS (MAKE TWO)
Note: The eyeballs can be knit on stitches picked up from the body, or knit separately and sewn on.

With white yarn, pick up 6 sts from the head using two needles held parallel—3 sts on each needle. (Alternatively cast on 6 sts.) Distribute on dpns and join into round, leaving a long yarn tail for sewing later.

Rnd 1: Knit.
Rnd 2: [K1, LLI] around—12 sts.
Rnds 3–5: Knit.
Rnd 6: K2tog around—6 sts.

Cut yarn, loosely draw through rem sts, stuff eyeball and pull tight. Weave in end. If making separately, close the cast-on opening and sew to front of head.

With black yarn or thread, embroider pupils by repeatedly stitching in and out of the same 2 sts until a roundish shape is achieved. Embroider mouth in a V shape.

ARMS (MAKE TWO)
Note: As with the eyes, the arms can be knit on stitches picked up from the body, or knit separately and sewn on.

Pick up 5 sts horizontally along the side of the body (or CO 5 sts if you want to knit the arms separately and sew them on).

Knit approx 10 rows of i-cord (add or subtract rows for longer/shorter arms). I recommend tugging the cord every row or two to close up the back of the cord.

Next Row: K2tog, k1, k2tog—3 sts.

Work picot bind off for the fingers as follows: *CO 3 sts (knitted cast on is recommended), BO 4 sts, put sts on RH needle back on LH needle, rep from * once more, then CO 3 sts, BO 4 sts, cut yarn and draw through rem st. Weave in end by drawing through the center of the cord and into the body.

BOOK
The pages and cover are worked flat. Slip the first stitch of every row knitwise.

With book cover yarn, CO 8 sts. Knit 12 rows. Purl 1 row. Knit 11 more rows.

BO all sts and weave in ends.

With white yarn, CO 7 sts. Knit 11 rows. Purl 1 row. Knit 10 more rows.

BO all sts and weave in ends.

Place the pages inside the cover, with the purl side of the page "spine" facing the knit side of the cover "spine." Stitch in place.

Abbreviations & Techniques

approx	approximately
beg	beginning
BH	buttonhole
BO	bind off (cast off)
cdd	central double decrease: slip 1 as if to knit, k2tog, pass slipped stitch over the k2tog and off needle
cddp	central double decrease purlwise: slip 1 as if to purl, p2tog, pass slipped stitch over the p2tog and off needle
CC	contrast color
ch	chain using crochet hook
CO	cast on
cont	continue / continuing
dec('d)	decrease / decreasing / decreased
dpn(s)	double pointed needle(s)
est	established
inc('d)	increase / increasing / increased
inc3	3-in-1 increase: (k1, yo, k1) all in the same stitch
inc5	5-in-1 increase: (k1, yo, k1, yo, k1) all in the same stitch
inc7	7-in-1 increase: (k1, yo, k1, yo, k1, yo, k1) all in the same stitch
k	knit
k2tog	knit two stitches together
k3tog	knit three stitches together
kfb	knit into front and back of stitch
L1	lifted increase: from front of work, lift st from row below onto left needle and knit
LH	left-hand
m	marker
m1	make 1 stitch

m1L	make 1 left: insert left needle under horizontal strand between st just worked and next st from the front to the back, knit through the back loop
m1p	make 1 purlwise: insert left needle, from front to back, under strand of yarn which runs between next stitch on left needle and last stitch on right needle; purl this stitch through back loop
m1R	make 1 right: insert left needle under horizontal strand between st just worked and next st from the back to the front, knit through the front loop
MC	main color
p	purl
p&b1	purl 1 stitch, then place a bead on it with your crochet hook
p2tog	purl two stitches together
p3tog	purl three stitches together
patt(s)	pattern(s)
pfb	purl into front and back of stitch
pm	place marker
psso	pass slipped stitches over
rem	remain(ing)
rep	repeat
rev St st	reverse stockinette stitch (stocking stitch)
RH	right-hand
RS	right side
rnd(s)	round(s)
s2kp	slip 2 stitches, knit 1, pass slipped sts over
sc	single crochet
skp	slip 1 knitwise, knit 1, pass slipped st over
sk2p	slip 1 knitwise, knit 2 together, pass slipped st over

sl m	slip marker
ssk	slip 2 sts individually as if to knit, then knit those 2 stitches together through the back loops
ssp	slip 2 sts individually as if to knit, then purl those 2 stitches together through the back loops
sl	slip
sl st	crochet slip stitch
st(s)	stitch(es)
St st	stockinette stitch (stocking stitch)

tbl	through the back loop
tog	together
w&t	wrap and turn (short rows)
WS	wrong side
wyib	with yarn in back
wyif	with yarn in front
yf	yarn forward: bring yarn between needles to front of work
yb	yarn back: take yarn between needles to back of work
yo	yarn over

About the Designers

Sarah Barbour has been designing knitwear since 2005. Her patterns have been published in *Interweave Knits, Knitscene, Interweave Crochet, YARN, Yarn Forward* and *Inside Crochet*; she has also worked with Knit Picks, Nashua and Classic Elite yarn companies. Before yarn took over her life, she received a Masters degree in Library and Information Science from the University of Illinois. She thinks every librarian should have a cape. Sarah can be found online at www.ropeknits.com or on Ravelry as Rope.

THE CONTRIBUTORS

Brenda K. B. Anderson makes mascots during the day. She cooks, knits, crochets, and belly dances at night. She can regularly be found hanging out in the 746.43 section of her local library. She lives in a little house in Saint Paul, MN, with her ridiculously good-looking husband and their hairy baby, Mr. Kittypants. Brenda can be found on Ravelry as yarnville.

Heather Broadhurst, self-proclaimed queen of short rows, has many a memory of studying, researching, reading and being hushed in library stacks. With a well-deserved reputation for knitting almost anything with almost anything (especially if there is math involved) when not playing with her computer network or tech writing/editing, she can be seen walking and knitting (yes, at the same time) in San Diego, California. Heather can be found online at walkaboutknitter.blogspot.com or on Ravelry as walkaboutknitter.

Kristen Hanley Cardozo is the daughter of a librarian, a bibliophile, and a yarn collector. She lives in the San Francisco Bay Area with her husband and three kids, writing and knitting or thinking about writing and knitting. You can follow her adventures and mishaps online at knittingkninja.com.

Brenda Castiel has been knitting on and off since she was in her teens, but became somewhat obsessed with it in 2007. She loves squishy wools for the short, mild Los Angeles winters, and likes cottons and blends for the rest of the year. Brenda firmly believes that even beginner knitters can create something beautiful and useful so she strives to keep patterns simple yet original. She has sold her designs to *Interweave Knits, Creative Knitting, KNIT magazine,* Classic Elite Yarns, Knit Picks, *Tangled* magazine, The Sanguine Gryphon, *Yarn* magazine, and Three Irish Girls Yarns. Brenda can be found online at knitandtravelandsuch.blogspot.com or on Ravelry as Goodstuff.

Holly Chayes is a New York-based knitter and designer. When she's not knitting, she can usually be found drinking far too much coffee, spinning, sewing, and working as a costume designer. Holly can be found online at hollychayes.wordpress.com.

Cheezombie, aka Kahra Graebner, often finds herself bleary eyed and finger sore, but still knitting and watching slasher movies and cartoons, at 2 a.m. The by-products of these late night sessions fuel others, whereby creating a cycle of sleeplessness and creativity and funny critters. She can be found on line at cheezombie.etsy.com or on Ravelry as (of all things) cheezombie.

Nina Machlin Dayton has been knitting, designing and teaching for 35 years. When she's not earning her living with knitting she works as a theatrical archivist/librarian. A native New Yorker, Nina now lives in western Massachusetts with her family, and with a number of books that many people think excessive, but which she deems not yet enough. We won't even talk about the yarn…. Find Nina online at ninaknits.wordpress.com or on Ravelry as ninaknits.

Susan Dittrich lives in Pittsburgh, PA, with her husband and an unruly stash of sock yarn. She does most of her knitting in coffee shops and on her bus commute to work. She is the founder of the Shadyside Stitch 'n Bitch group. Her most popular designs have been published in Knitty.com and *Interweave Knits*. Susan can be found online her at handknitsbysusan.wordpress.com or on Ravelry as handknitsbysusan.

Rachel Erin believes in making every day as beautiful as possible, and believes that making and doing things by hand have a special ability to make an ordinary day beautiful. She loves knits that are special yet versatile, memorable yet classic, and as enjoyable to wear as they are to knit. Rachel can be found online at www.rachelerin.com or on Ravelry as racherin.

Carol Feller is an independent knitwear designer and knitting teacher. Her patterns for men, women, and children are widely published in books and magazines, including *Knitting in the Sun* (Wiley, 2009), Twist Collective, *Interweave Knits,* and Knitty. She lives in Cork, Ireland, with her husband, four sons, and a large dog. Her new book, *Contemporary Irish Knits,* was published by Wiley in August 2011. Carol can be found on line at www.stolenstitches.com and on Ravelry as Littlefellers.

Sharon Fuller works as a database developer and enjoys designing knitting patterns as another sort of programming. She brings a dressmaker's eye for detail and a love of surface decoration to her designs. Sharon is a frequent contributor to Cooperative Press books, and has designed for Twist Collective, *Interweave Knits,* and others. Find her on Ravelry as sharonf.

Joy Gerhardt is an American knitter living in the UK. On a lark one day, she grabbed some yarn and needles, and it all went downhill from there. Now she knits, spins, designs, and spends many, many hours on Ravelry. Her favorite authors include D. H. Lawrence, Philip Pullman, and Nick Hornby. Upon entering a library, she always makes a beeline for the language and linguistics section (DDC 400) and then the needlearts section (DDC 746). Joy can be found online at joyarna.blogspot.com or on Ravelry as Joyuna.

Meghan Jones has a BFA in fibers and textiles. She lives in Spokane with her two daughters, Hubs the Great, and her yarn stash. Meghan can be found online at www.littlenutmegproductions.blogspot.com, or on Ravelry as anythingbutsnow.

Molly Kent is a teacher and artisan papermaker from Seattle. She draws inspiration from science, history, and the natural world. Plus she just likes making stuff, the more challenging the better. Molly can be found online at www.WFTR.biz or on Ravelry as beadskater.

James Magee has taken up a challenge: whenever male knitters complain that there are no fun patterns for men, people tell them to design their own, so that is exactly what James decided to do. He now designs knitwear in addition to experimenting in crochet and spinning. He lives in Montreal, Quebec, where he also works and studies in science education. James can be found online at jamesknits.tumblr.com or on Ravelry as mymaille.

Kendra Nitta's first job was shelving books in the 600s and 700 sections of the Orange County Public Library in southern California. She's now a member of the Friends of the Pasadena Public Library and still an avid reader. In addition to knitting, she sews, quilts, and reviews the books in her own craft book library. You can find her online at www.missknitta.com.

Heather Ordover transitioned into writing full time after ten years an award-winning New York City high school teacher and university professor. Her latest joy has been writing and editing the second pattern book in the series *What Would Madame Defarge Knit? Creations Inspired by Classic Characters.* She currently hosts her own long-running podcast, CraftLit: A Podcast for Crafters Who Love Books (think "audiobook with benefits"). Her crafty writing has appeared in *Spin-Off, WeaveZine,* and *Cast-on,* and her design graces the cover of *Knitting Socks from Around the World.* She currently writes and designs in Northern Virginia where she lives with her amused husband, two goofy sons, and far too many devoted mosquitoes. Oh, and she knits.

Theressa Silver took up knitting because she was tired of being haunted by her grandmother's needles, which were sitting, loved but unused, on a shelf. Having a science background, she quickly fell in love with the mathematical and technical aspects of knitting. She has been designing and sewing clothes for most of her life and discovered that the flexibility and shape-ability of knit fabric opens up a whole new realm of possibilities and inspires her to test limits and create the unexpected. She lives in Oregon with her husband, son, five cats, and a dog, all of whom participate one way or another in the knitting process. Theressa can be found on Ravelry as argentgal.

Kristen TenDyke is a knit and crochet designer from Maine. She loves playing with yarn and has published designs in *Interweave Knits, Interweave Crochet, Vogue Knitting, Knit Simple,* Twist Collective, and Knitty.com. She has also worked with various yarn companies such as Quince & Co., Berroco and Classic Elite Yarns. In 2010 Kristen began a growing collection of designs that are dedicated to supporting the use and production of eco-friendly yarns. Her Caterpillar Knits designs use organic, fair trade, low carbon footprint, recycled, animal friendly or vegan yarns that use low impact, natural dyes, or none at all. You can find Kristen online at www.kristentendyke.com and www.caterpillarknits.com.

Alex Tinsley like simple textures and interesting shapes, soft wools and kettle dyes. Ice cream. Addis. Hats. Spinning. Ducklings. (She's not much for bio-writing, though.) Alex has an under-utilized degree in psychology and has been knitting since about 2004 and designing almost as long. She's had patterns published in Knitty, *Knit Simple,* and *Interweave Knits,* though she primarily self-publishes. She owns approximately 60 hats at this time. You can find her online at www.dull-roar.com.

Karin Wilmoth teaches knitting at Anacapa Fine Yarns in Ventura, CA, and is a homeschooling mom. She began her knitting journey 11 years ago in an insane attempt to knit socks (nine pairs—her first projects ever) for her whole family in three months. Her natural ability to teach, combined with her nerdy love of math, humor, and science, and her love of fine details inspire her to explore unusual knitting constructions. Whether it is top-down, sideways, circular, or otherwise geometrical, she enjoys creating knits that offer a different perspective. Find her musings and other knitterly ponderings at knittingkirigami.wordpress.com.

Acknowledgments

In any book, but especially a multi-contributor project like this one, credit is due to so many people and organizations that it might be impossible to list them all but I've made a stab at it anyway. If I've inadvertently left anyone out, please believe the omission is due to a faulty memory rather than a lack of gratitude.

To Stephannie Tallent, Katherine Vaughan, Alex Tinsley, Rachel Hosting, Nina Dayton, and Jenn Wisbeck for providing initial encouragement and support for this project when it was still a crazy little germ of an idea;

To been-there-done-that authors Larrisa Brown, Genevieve Miller, and Heather Ordover, who were kind enough to share their book-writing experiences with a nosy stranger;

To the Camden Carroll Library at Morehead State University, and in particular Rob Sammons, who shepherded my request for the vintage photograph that appears at the front of this book—Rob, you're a credit to your profession;

To Jay Petersen, for generously allowing us to use his mosaic alphabet chart;

To Meghan Jones, who went above and beyond and contributed all the schematics for the patterns in this book;

To the Cleveland Public Library for graciously allowing us to use its beautiful building for the photoshoot;

To all the fabulous designers who contributed to this book, waited patiently for their yarn, and took editorial suggestions in stride: you guys rock! You've been a joy to work with and I am proud to be associated with every single one of these designs;

To the yarn companies that have been so generous in their support of this project: Alpha B Yarn, Artfibers, Becoming Art, Blue Sky Alpacas/Spud & Chloë, Brooklyn Tweed, Brown Sheep, Cascade Yarns, Handmaiden, Knit Picks, Knitting Fever, St. Denis, Three Irish Girls, Yarn Love, WEBS/Valley Yarns, and Westminster Fibers—may your yarns be ever as beautiful and your staff be ever as patient!;

To Shannon Okey, for boundless enthusiasm, plenty of encouragement, and ridiculous amounts of cheerfulness and patience;

To Elizabeth Green Musselman, without whose organizational and administrative skills—and above all, patience—this book would never have happened;

To my mother, who shares my love of knitting and has never failed to encourage my wild schemes;

To my children, who have heard the phrase, "Not now, I'm knitting!" far more than is fair, and to my husband, who's been proofreader, cheerleader, sounding board, and tech support for this and many other projects—thanks, guys. I love you.

About Cooperative Press
PARTNERS IN PUBLISHING

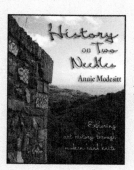

Cooperative Press (formerly anezka media) was founded in 2007 by Shannon Okey, a voracious reader as well as writer and editor, who had been doing freelance acquisitions work, introducing authors with projects she believed in to editors at various publishers.

Although working with traditional publishers can be very rewarding, there are some books that fly under their radar. They're too avant-garde, or the marketing department doesn't know how to sell them, or they don't think they'll sell 50,000 copies in a year.

5,000 or 50,000. Does the book matter to that 5,000? Then it should be published.

In 2009, Cooperative Press changed its named to reflect the relationships we have developed with authors working on books. We work together to put out the best quality books we can, and share in the proceeds accordingly.

Thank you for supporting independent publishers and authors.

We're on Ravelry as CooperativePress. Please join our low-volume mailing list and check out our other books at...

WWW.COOPERATIVEPRESS.COM

CPSIA information can be obtained at www.ICGtesting.com
Printed in the USA
LVOW05s1439280415

436412LV00005B/16/P

9 781937 513238